· MACMILLAN / McGRAW · HILL ·

MATH ANTHO

STORIES,
POEMS,
& SONGS

GRADES
KINDERGARTEN
1 AND 2

MACMILLAN / McGRAW-HILL
SCHOOL PUBLISHING COMPANY

New York   Columbus

I Can!

MATH ACTIVITY PROGRAM

Mathematics
in Action

The **MATH ANTHOLOGY** Stories, Poems, and Songs offers a variety of traditional and contemporary selections of children's literature. These selections are used as the basis for many of the individual and small-group activities in MATHEMATICS IN ACTION.

A *Read-Aloud Selections* audiocassette of the literature that opens each chapter and a *Math Songs* audiocassette containing all the songs in the **MATH ANTHOLOGY** are provided with the program.

Correlation to *Mathematics in Action* 1994 and *I Can! Math Activity Program:* The chart on pages xii-xvii keys every story, poem, and song to an activity in the *I Can! Math Activity Program* and correlates each selection for use across the grades where appropriate. In addition, every story, poem, and song is correlated to the 1994 *MATHEMATICS IN ACTION* program. The Mathematics and Literature logo in the Teacher's Edition identifies the lesson in which a selection is used.

1994 Printing
Copyright © 1993 Macmillan/McGraw-Hill School Publishing Company

MACMILLAN/McGRAW-HILL SCHOOL DIVISION
10 UNION SQUARE EAST, NEW YORK, NEW YORK 10003

Printed in the United States of America

ISBN 0-02-109095-5 / K-2

7 8 9 BAW 99 98 97 96 95 94

Illustration Credits: Lauren Rosenblum, Ed Phillips, Joe Waves, Circa 86, Paul Harvey, Joan Holub, Melanie Hope Greenberg

Cover & Text Design: Circa 86

Cover Illustration: Circa 86

ACKNOWLEDGMENTS

The publisher gratefully acknowledges permission to reprint the following copyrighted material:

ANNICK PRESS LTD.
MOIRA'S BIRTHDAY by Robert Munsch. Text copyright © 1987 by Robert Munsch. Art copyright © 1987 by Michael Martichenko. Reprinted by permission of Annick Press Ltd.

BANTAM BOOKS
ANNIE'S PET by Barbara Brenner. Text Copyright © 1989 by Bank Street College of Education. Used by permission of Bantam Books, a division of Bantam Doubleday Dell Publishing Group, Inc.

BYRD BAYLOR
"Why Coyote Isn't Blue" retold by Noel Roubidoux, Pima, St. John's School from AND IT IS STILL THAT WAY by Byrd Baylor. Copyright © 1976 by Byrd Baylor. Published by Trail's West Press, Santa Fe, New Mexico. Reprinted by permission of the author.

CURTIS BROWN LTD.
COULDN'T WE HAVE A TURTLE INSTEAD? by Judith Vigna. Copyright © 1975 by Judith Vigna. Reprinted by permission of Curtis Brown, Ltd.

"The Face of the Clock" from WONDERFUL TIME by Phyllis McGinley. Copyright © 1965, 1966 by Phyllis McGinley. Reprinted by permission of Curtis Brown, Ltd.

LAURA CECIL, Literary Agent For Children's Books
"Animals' Houses" from THE WANDERING MOON AND OTHER POEMS by James Reeves (Puffin Books). Reprinted by permission of The James Reeves Estate.

THE CHILD'S WORLD
HOW MANY WAYS CAN YOU CUT A PIE? by Jane Belk Moncure. Copyright © The Child's World, Inc., Elgin, IL and used with their permission.

HARPERCOLLINS PUBLISHERS, INC.
Excerpt from "Square as a House" from DOGS AND DRAGONS/TREES AND DREAMS by Karla Kuskin. Copyright © 1980 by Karla Kuskin.

"Okay Everybody" from NEAR THE WINDOW TREE by Karla Kuskin. Copyright © 1975 by Karla Kuskin.

"A List" from FROG AND TOAD TOGETHER by Arnold Lobel. Copyright © 1972 by Arnold Lobel.

"The Crickets" from MOUSE SOUP by Arnold Lobel. Copyright © 1977 by Arnold Lobel.

ALL OF OUR NOSES ARE HERE AND OTHER NOODLE TALES by Alvin Schwartz. Text copyright © 1985 by Alvin Schwartz.

"Band-Aids" from WHERE THE SIDEWALK ENDS by Shel Silverstein. Copyright © 1974 by Evil Eye Music, Inc.

"Homework Machine" from A LIGHT IN THE ATTIC by Shel Silverstein. Copyright © 1981 by Evil Eye Music, Inc.

CAPS FOR SALE by Esphyr Slobodkina. © 1940 and 1947, © renewed 1968 by Esphyr Slobodkina.

MORRIS GOES TO SCHOOL by B. Wiseman. Copyright © 1970 by B. Wiseman.

All are reprinted by permission of HarperCollins Publishers, Inc.

(Acknowledgments continue on page 217)

•CONTENTS•

KINDERGARTEN

Harvest
a Danish folk song 2

Cats
a poem by Eleanor Farjeon 3

The Mitten
a Ukrainian folktale retold by Alvin Tresselt 4

Hokey Pokey
an American singing game 7

Caps for Sale
a story by Esphyr Slobodkina 8

There are Big Waves
a poem by Eleanor Farjeon 11

What is Pink?
a poem by Christina Rossetti 12

Hello Song
a traditional song 13

Too Much Noise
a story by Ann McGovern 14

Little Fish
a poem selected and translated from Spanish by Margot C. Griego,
Betsy L. Bucks, Sharon S. Gilbert, and Laurel H. Kimball 19

If You're Happy
a traditional song **20**

Hattie and the Fox
a story by Mem Fox **21**

Draw a Bucket of Water
an African American play party game **24**

Couldn't We Have a Turtle Instead?
a story by Judith Vigna **26**

Okay Everybody
a poem by Karla Kuskin **28**

Over in the Meadow
a traditional song **29**

A Counting Rhyme
a poem by M. M. Stephenson **31**

Hurry, Little Pony
a Spanish folk song **32**

Tatum's Favorite Shape
a story by Dorothy Thole **33**

Square as a House
a poem by Karla Kuskin **36**

Two Greedy Bears
a Hungarian folktale retold by Mirra Ginsburg **37**

Jesse Bear, What Will you Wear?
a story by Nancy White Carlstrom **40**

Money's Funny
a poem by Mary Ann Hoberman **43**

Peanut Butter
a camp song.. 44

Who Has the Penny?
a traditional song... 46

Annie's Pet
a story by Barbara Brenner.................................. 47

Three Little Monkeys
a traditional rhyme... 49

Moira's Birthday
a story by Robert Munsch................................... 50

Too Many Daves
a poem by Dr. Seuss.. 53

One, Two, Buckle My Shoe
a traditional rhyme... 54

Going over the Sea
a Canadian street rhyme.................................... 55

GRADE 1

All of Our Noses Are Here
a story retold by Alvin Schwartz........................... 58

Counting Song
a Mexican folk song.. 60

Who Wants One?
a story by Mary Serfozo.................................... 61

This Old Man
an English folk song.. 63

The Enormous Turnip
a Russian folktale retold by Kathy Parkinson............... 64

The Graceful Elephant
a rhyme from Mexico selected by Lulu Delacre **66**

Johnny Works with One Hammer
an American singing game **67**

Five Little Ducks
a counting song by Raffi **68**

Five Brown Teddies
a traditional rhyme **70**

The Cats of Kilkenny
a traditional rhyme **71**

There Were Two Wrens
a traditional rhyme **72**

The Crickets
from *Mouse Soup* by Arnold Lobel **73**

The Creature in the Classroom
a poem by Jack Prelutsky **75**

Chook, Chook, Chook
a traditional rhyme **76**

Ten Little Fingers
a traditional song **77**

Ten in a Bed
a song by Mary Rees **78**

Mexicali Soup
a story by Kathryn Hitte and William D. Hayes **80**

Ten Puppies (Diez Perritos)
a Puerto Rican folk song **85**

Bleezer's Ice Cream
from *The New Kid on the Block* by Jack Prelutsky **86**

Hugs and Kisses
a rhyme by Charlotte Pomerantz................................... 88

The Ants at the Olympics
a poem by Richard Digance 89

Mud for⤬ Sale
a story by Brenda Nelson 91

A Poem for a Pickle
a poem by Eve Merriam 93

Fifteen Cents
a traditional rhyme.. 94

Pop Goes the Weasel
an American singing game... 95

Two Loaves
from *I Did It* by Harlow Rockwell 96

Spring Is Coming
a song by Milton Kaye 97

The Knee-High Man
an African American folktale retold by Julius Lester 98

Morris Goes to School
a story by B. Wiseman 100

Cottage
a poem by Eleanor Farjeon 104

A List
from *Frog and Toad Together* by Arnold Lobel 105

The Oak Tree
a story by Laura Jane Coats 108

The Face of the Clock
a poem by Phyllis McGinley 110

Ai Hai Yo
a Shansi melody from China 112

The Most Wonderful Egg in the World
a story by Helme Heine 113

Animals' Houses
a poem by James Reeves 115

Too Many Hopkins
a story by Tomie dePaola 116

Why Coyote Isn't Blue
from *And It Is Still That Way*, Legends told by Arizona Indian Children
with notes by Byrd Baylor, retold by Noel Roubidoux, Pima, St. John's School 118

Band-Aids
a poem by Shel Silverstein from *Where the Sidewalk Ends* 120

The Marrog
a poem by R. C. Scriven 121

Leopard Finds Gold
a West African folktale retold by Mary Pat Champeau 123

GRADE 2

The Banza
a Haitian story told by Diane Wolkstein 128

There Was an Old Man with a Beard
a poem by Edward Lear 132

There Was an Old Man Who Said
an anonymous poem 133

Five Fat Turkeys
a traditional song 134

The Story Snail
a story by Anne Rockwell 135

A Birthday Basket for Tía
a story by Pat Mora 140

Song of the Dragon
a traditional Chinese folk song 143

Homework Machine
a poem by Shel Silverstein from *A Light in the Attic* 144

A Thousand Pails of Water
a Japanese story by Ronald Roy 145

Don't Ask Me
a poem by Yolanda Nave 148

Penelope Gets Wheels
a story by Esther Allen Peterson 149

Hot Cross Buns
a traditional song 151

How Big Is a Foot?
a story by Rolf Myller 152

A New Coat for Anna
a story by Harriet Ziefert 154

Spring in China
a Chinese folk song 157

Ninety-Nine Pockets
a story by Jean Myrick 158

A Hot Thirsty Day
a story by Marjorie Weinman Sharmat 162

Using Subtraction
by Lee Blair from *Arithmetic in Verse and Rhyme* 166

Clocks and More Clocks
a story by Pat Hutchins 167

New Bicycle
a poem by Yolanda Nave **169**

Maxie
a story by Mildred Kantrowitz **170**

All Who Born in January
a folk song from Trinidad **173**

Two Hundred Rabbits
a story by Lonzo Anderson and Adrienne Adams **174**

The Snow Parade
a story by Barbara Brenner **179**

Surprises
by Jean Conder Soule from *The Random House Book of Poetry for Children* **182**

The Village of Round and Square Houses
a story by Ann Grifalconi **183**

How Many Ways Can You Cut a Pie?
a story by Jane Belk Moncure **189**

A Sum
a poem by Lewis Carroll **192**

The Doorbell Rang
a story by Pat Hutchins **193**

Ten Little Squirrels
a traditional rhyme **195**

Hop Up, My Ladies
an American folk song **196**

Too Many Books!
a story by Caroline Feller Bauer **198**

Bit by Bit
a story by Lisa Yount **200**

USING
MATH ANTHOLOGY

This chart offers a correlation of the Anthology selections to the Math Activity Program for Kindergarten and Grades 1 and 2. Bold face type indicates where the story, poem, or song is used in the Teacher's Guide of the program.

SELECTION	PAGE	KINDERGARTEN	GRADE 1	GRADE 2
Harvest a Danish folk song	2	**Starting Out**		Chapter 8
Cats a poem	3	**Chapter 1**		
The Mitten a Ukrainian folktale	4	**Chapter 1** Chapter 4 Chapter 6 Chapter 9	Chapter 1 Chapter 4 Chapter 5	Chapter 1
Hokey Pokey an American singing game	7	**Chapter 1**		
Caps for Sale a story	8	Chapter 1 **Chapter 2**	Chapter 7	Chapter 4
There are Big Waves a poem	11	**Chapter 2**		
What is Pink? a poem	12	**Chapter 2**		
Hello Song a traditional song	13	**Chapter 2** Chapter 3		
Too Much Noise a story	14	**Chapter 3** Chapter 6	Chapter 1 Chapter 4 Chapter 5	Chapter 1
Little Fish a poem	19	**Chapter 3**		
If You're Happy a traditional song	20	**Chapter 3**		
Hattie and the Fox a story	21	**Chapter 4** Chapter 9	Chapter 2 Chapter 3	
Draw a Bucket of Water an African American play party game	24	**Chapter 4**		
Couldn't We Have a Turtle Instead? a story	26	**Chapter 5**	Chapter 9 Chapter 11	Chapter 3 Chapter 10

SELECTION	PAGE	KINDERGARTEN	GRADE 1	GRADE 2
Okay Everybody a poem	28	**Chapter 5**	Chapter 8	Chapter 5
Over in the Meadow a traditional song	29	**Chapter 6**	Chapter 1 Chapter 6	
A Counting Rhyme a poem	31	**Chapter 6** Chapter 9	Chapter 1 Chapter 4 Chapter 9 Chapter 12	Chapter 1 Chapter 12
Hurry, Little Pony a Spanish folk song	32	**Chapter 6**	Chapter 1	
Tatum's Favorite Shape a story	33	**Chapter 7**	Chapter 11	Chapter 10 Chapter 11
Square as a House a poem	36	Chapter 2 **Chapter 7**	Chapter 11	Chapter 10
Two Greedy Bears a Hungarian folktale	37	Chapter 5 **Chapter 7**	Chapter 8 Chapter 11	Chapter 5 Chapter 11
Jesse Bear, What Will You Wear? a story	40	**Chapter 8**	Chapter 10	
Money's Funny a poem	43	**Chapter 8**	Chapter 7	Chapter 4
Peanut Butter a camp song	44	**Chapter 8**	Chapter 10	
Who Has the Penny? a traditional song	46	**Chapter 8**	Chapter 7	Chapter 4
Annie's Pet a story	47	**Chapter 9**	Chapter 2 Chapter 3	Chapter 4
Three Little Monkeys a traditional rhyme	49	**Chapter 9**	Chapter 2 Chapter 3	
Moira's Birthday a story	50	Chapter 6 **Chapter 10**	Chapter 1 Chapter 10	Chapter 8 Chapter 9
Too Many Daves a poem	53	**Chapter 10**	Chapter 6	
One, Two, Buckle My Shoe a traditional rhyme	54	**Chapter 10**	Chapter 1	
Going over the Sea a Canadian street rhyme	55	Chapter 4 Chapter 6 **Chapter 10**	Chapter 1	
All of Our Noses Are Here a story	58	Chapter 4	**Chapter 1**	

SELECTION	PAGE	KINDERGARTEN	GRADE 1	GRADE 2
Counting Song a Mexican folk song	60	Chapter 6	**Chapter 1**	
Who Wants One? a story	61	Chapter 4 Chapter 6	**Chapter 1**	
This Old Man an English folk song	63	Chapter 6	**Chapter 1**	
The Enormous Turnip a Russian folktale	64	Chapter 9	**Chapter 2**	
The Graceful Elephant a rhyme from Mexico	66	Chapter 4 Chapter 9	**Chapter 2** Chapter 3	
Johnny Works with One Hammer an American singing game	67	Chapter 4 Chapter 9	**Chapter 2**	
Five Little Ducks a counting song	68	Chapter 9	**Chapter 3**	
Five Brown Teddies a traditional rhyme	70	Chapter 9	**Chapter 3**	
The Cats of Kilkenny a traditional rhyme	71		**Chapter 3**	
There Were Two Wrens a traditional rhyme	72	Chapter 4 Chapter 9	**Chapter 3**	
The Crickets a story	73	Chapter 6	Chapter 1 **Chapter 4**	Chapter 1
The Creature in the Classroom a poem	75		**Chapter 4** Chapter 5	Chapter 1 Chapter 8
Chook, Chook, Chook a traditional rhyme	76		**Chapter 4** Chapter 9	Chapter 1
Ten Little Fingers a traditional song	77	Chapter 6 Chapter 9	Chapter 1 **Chapter 4** Chapter 5	Chapter 1
Ten in a Bed a song	78	Chapter 4 Chapter 6	Chapter 1 **Chapter 5**	Chapter 1
Mexicali Soup a story	80	Chapter 9	**Chapter 5**	Chapter 1
Ten Puppies (Diez Perritos) a Puerto Rican folk song	85	Chapter 6	Chapter 1 **Chapter 5**	Chapter 1
Bleezer's Ice Cream a poem	86	Chapter 10	**Chapter 6** Chapter 13	Chapter 6
Hugs and Kisses a rhyme	88	Chapter 10	**Chapter 6** Chapter 10	Chapter 8

SELECTION	PAGE	KINDERGARTEN	GRADE 1	GRADE 2
The Ants at the Olympics a poem	89		**Chapter 6** Chapter 10	Chapter 5 Chapter 8 Chapter 9
Mud for Sale a story	91	Chapter 8 Chapter 9	Chapter 4 **Chapter 7** Chapter 9 Chapter 13	Chapter 4 Chapter 12
A Poem for a Pickle a poem	93	Chapter 8	**Chapter 7**	Chapter 4
Fifteen Cents a traditional rhyme	94		**Chapter 7** Chapter 12	Chapter 3 Chapter 4
Pop Goes the Weasel an American singing game	95	Chapter 8	Chapter 4 Chapter 5 **Chapter 7**	Chapter 1 Chapter 4
Two Loaves a story	96		**Chapter 8** Chapter 10 Chapter 11	Chapter 5 Chapter 8 Chapter 10
Spring Is Coming a song	97	Starting Out	**Chapter 8**	Chapter 5 Chapter 8
The Knee-High Man an African American folktale	98	Chapter 5	**Chapter 8**	Chapter 5
Morris Goes to School a story	100	Chapter 6 Chapter 8	Chapter 1 Chapter 7 **Chapter 9**	Chapter 3 Chapter 4
Cottage a poem	104	Chapter 10	**Chapter 9**	Chapter 3
A List a story	105	Chapter 8	**Chapter 10**	
The Oak Tree a story	108	Chapter 8	**Chapter 10**	Chapter 8
The Face of the Clock a poem	110		**Chapter 10**	Chapter 8
Ai Hai Yo a Shansi melody from China	112		**Chapter 10**	Chapter 8
The Most Wonderful Egg in the World a story	113		Chapter 8 **Chapter 11**	Chapter 5 Chapter 10
Animals' Houses a poem	115	Chapter 7	**Chapter 11**	Chapter 10
Too Many Hopkins a story	116	Chapter 10	**Chapter 12** Chapter 13	Chapter 3 Chapter 12

SELECTION	PAGE	KINDERGARTEN	GRADE 1	GRADE 2
Why Coyote Isn't Blue a Native American folktale	118		Chapter 10 **Chapter 12** Chapter 13	Chapter 3 Chapter 8 Chapter 12
Band-Aids a poem	120		Chapter 6 **Chapter 13**	Chapter 6 Chapter 7
The Marrog a poem	121	Chapter 10	Chapter 8 **Chapter 13**	Chapter 5 Chapter 6 Chapter 7
Leopard Finds Gold a West African folktale	123	Chapter 10	**Chapter 13**	Chapter 6 Chapter 7 Chapter 12
The Banza a Haitian story	128	Chapter 6	Chapter 1 Chapter 4	**Chapter 1**
There Was an Old Man with a Beard a poem	132		Chapter 4	**Chapter 1**
There Was an Old Man Who Said a poem	133		Chapter 4 Chapter 9	**Chapter 1**
Five Fat Turkeys a traditional song	134	Chapter 4	Chapter 2 Chapter 3	**Chapter 1**
The Story Snail a story	135		Chapter 6	**Chapter 2**
A Birthday Basket for Tía a story set in Mexico	140		Chapter 6	**Chapter 2**
Song of the Dragon a traditional Chinese folk song	143		Chapter 6 Chapter 10	**Chapter 2** Chapter 8
Homework Machine a poem	144		Chapter 7 Chapter 9 Chapter 12	**Chapter 3** Chapter 4
A Thousand Pails of Water a story set in Japan	145		Chapter 12	**Chapter 3** **Chapter 9**
Don't Ask Me a poem	148	Chapter 9	Chapter 5 Chapter 12 Chapter 13	Chapter 1 **Chapter 3** Chapter 12
Penelope Gets Wheels a story	149			**Chapter 4**
Hot Cross Buns a traditional song	151	Chapter 8	Chapter 7	**Chapter 4**
How Big Is a Foot? a story	152		Chapter 8	**Chapter 5**
A New Coat for Anna a story	154		Chapter 8 Chapter 10	**Chapter 5** Chapter 8
Spring in China a Chinese folk song	157	Starting Out	Chapter 8 Chapter 10	**Chapter 5** Chapter 8

SELECTION	PAGE	KINDERGARTEN	GRADE 1	GRADE 2
Ninety-Nine Pockets a story	158		Chapter 6 Chapter 11 Chapter 13	Chapter 2 **Chapter 6** Chapter 10
A Hot Thirsty Day a story	162		Chapter 7 Chapter 12 Chapter 13	Chapter 4 **Chapter 6** **Chapter 7** Chapter 12
Using Subtraction a poem	166		Chapter 9 Chapter 12	**Chapter 7**
Clocks and More Clocks a story	167			**Chapter 8**
New Bicycle a poem	169	Chapter 10	Chapter 10	**Chapter 8**
Maxie a story	170		Chapter 10 Chapter 12	Chapter 3 **Chapter 8**
All Who Born In January a folk song from Trinidad	173		Chapter 10	**Chapter 8**
Two Hundred Rabbits a story	174			**Chapter 9**
The Snow Parade a story	179	Chapter 6	Chapter 1 Chapter 4 Chapter 6	Chapter 1 Chapter 2 Chapter 6 **Chapter 9**
Surprises a poem	182	Chapter 2	Chapter 11	**Chapter 10**
The Village of Round and Square Houses an African story	183		Chapter 11	**Chapter 10**
How Many Ways Can You Cut a Pie? a story	189		Chapter 11	**Chapter 11**
A Sum a poem	192		Chapter 11	**Chapter 11**
The Doorbell Rang a story	193	Chapter 10	Chapter 9 Chapter 13	Chapter 3 **Chapter 12**
Ten Little Squirrels a traditional rhyme	195		Chapter 4 Chapter 5 Chapter 13	Chapter 1 **Chapter 12**
Hop Up, My Ladies an American folk song	196		Chapter 13	**Chapter 12**
Too Many Books! a story	198			Chapter 4 **Chapter 13**
Bit by Bit a story	200			Chapter 4 **Chapter 13**

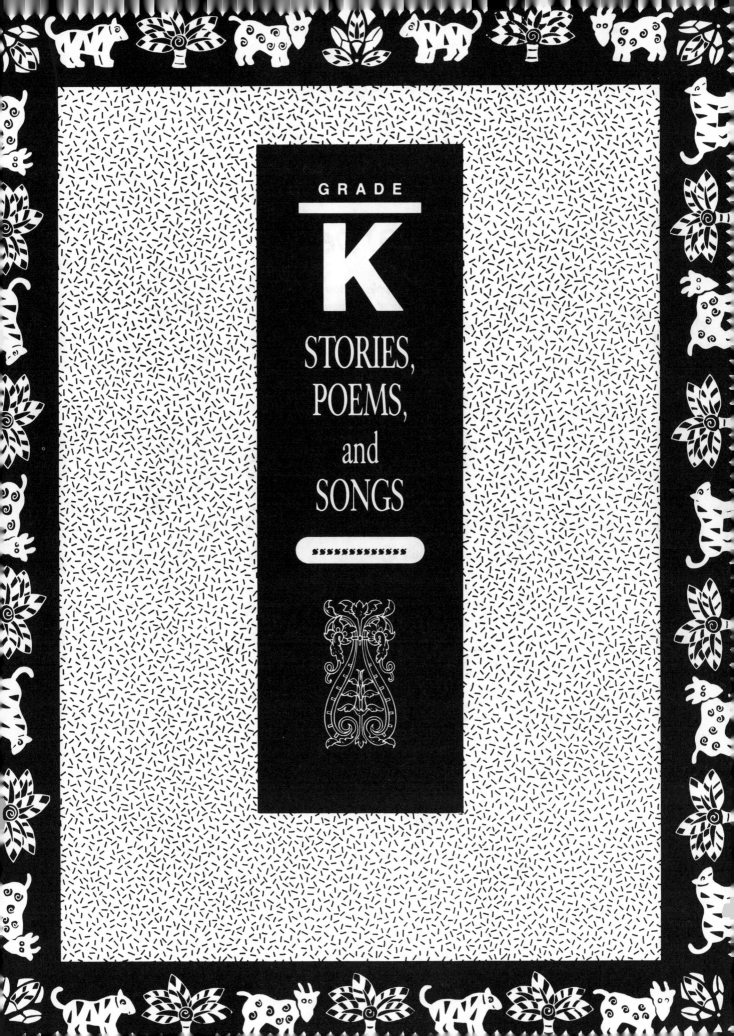

GRADE

K

STORIES, POEMS, and SONGS

Use with Grade K, Starting Out

 Math Songs
Side 1, Selection 1

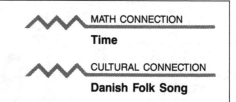
MATH CONNECTION
Time

CULTURAL CONNECTION
Danish Folk Song

Harvest

Autumn is the time for harvesting apples. In this Danish folk song, the changing color of the leaves also means a changing of the season. What other things remind children of autumn?

Danish Folk Song
Words Adapted

When all the leaves are turn - ing brown

and ap - ple trees are bend - ing down,

It's time to pick the ap - ples sweet

and gath - er in the har - vest.

Come and pick the ap - ples sweet,

ap - ples sweet, ap - ples sweet.

Reach up high and don't be shy or

you will be the last to eat.

2

Cats

BY ELEANOR FARJEON

Where do cats sleep? Anywhere! On top of things, in the middle—anywhere. This poem can serve as a good introduction to positional terms.

Cats sleep
Anywhere,
Any table,
Any chair,
Top of piano,
Window-ledge,
In the middle,
On the edge,
Open drawer,
Empty shoe,
Anybody's
Lap will do,
Fitted in a
Cardboard box,
In the cupboard
With your frocks—
Anywhere!
They don't care!
Cats sleep
Anywhere.

MATH CONNECTIONS

Positioning
Counting
Adding
Subtracting

CULTURAL CONNECTION

Ukrainian Folktale

The Mitten

A UKRAINIAN FOLKTALE RETOLD BY ALVIN TRESSELT

The Mitten, a Ukrainian folktale retold by Alvin Tresselt, can be used to illustrate inside *and* outside, *as well as counting to 8 and adding and subtracting.*

*I*t was the coldest day of the winter, and a little boy was trudging through the forest gathering firewood for his grandmother.

"Bring back all you can find," the old woman had said as she sat knitting a pair of mittens. "The north wind blows cold, and we must have a good fire to keep us warm."

All morning the boy worked, picking up sticks, until his sled was well loaded. Then a very strange thing happened. Just as he picked up the last stick he dropped one of his mittens in the snow.

Now, how a boy could do this on the coldest day of winter I'll never know, but that's the way my grandfather tells the story.

Off he went with his load of wood, and the mitten was left lying on a snowdrift.

As soon as he was out of sight a little mouse came scurrying through the woods. She was very cold, and when she spied the little boy's mitten with its feathery fur cuff, she popped right in to get warm. It was just the right size for a tiny mouse.

Presently a green frog came hip-hopping over the snow.

"Anybody home?" she asked when she saw the mitten.

"Only me," said the mouse, "and come in quickly before you freeze."

They had no sooner settled themselves snugly in the red wool lining when an owl flew down.

"May I join you in that lovely mitten?" he asked.

"If you mind your manners," replied the mouse, for owls always made her nervous.

"And don't wiggle around too much," added the frog, "because it's a bit tight in here."

It wasn't long before a rabbit came down the forest path.

"Is there any room for me in that nice warm mitten?" asked the rabbit. "It's awfully cold out here."

"Not much space left," said the mouse and the frog and the owl. "But come in. We'll see what we can do."

Even before the rabbit had gotten herself tucked in, a fox trotted up to the mitten, and after a good deal of trouble she got herself in with the others. The mouse was beginning to think maybe she shouldn't have been so generous, but with the bitter wind outside, what else could she do?

And now, as if things weren't bad enough, the next visitor was a big gray wolf who wanted to come in, too. "I don't know how we'll manage it," said the mouse, "But we'll try."

Everyone moved around a bit, and finally the wolf was squeezed into the mitten. It was very crowded by now, but at least it was warm.

Things had just gotten arranged nicely when the animals heard a great snorting. It was a wild boar, and he was very anxious to get in out of the wind.

"Oh, dear!" cried the little mouse, for the mitten was already beginning to stretch a little. "We just don't have any more room!"

"I'll be very careful," said the boar. With that he squinched himself into the mitten along with the mouse and the frog, the owl, the rabbit, the fox and the wolf. I know this because my grandfather told me.

But the worst was yet to come, for who should appear now but a bear! He was very big and very cold.

"No room! No room!" cried the animals even before the bear had a chance to speak.

"Nonsense!" said the bear.

"There's always room for one more." And, without so much as a please or thank you, he began crawling into the mitten. He put his paw in first, and the mitten creaked and groaned. He put his other paw in and one of the seams popped. Then he took a big breath and pushed himself in.

Now while all this was going on, along came a little black cricket. She was very old, and her creaky legs ached with the cold. When she saw the mitten she said to herself, "Now that looks like a nice warm place. I'll just hop over and see if I can squeeze in too!"

But, ah me, that's all that was needed to finish off the poor old mitten. The cricket had no more than put her first scratchy foot inside when, with a rip and a snap, the stitches came apart, the old leather cracked and the soft red lining split in half, popping all the animals into the snow!

Well at this very moment the little boy discovered that he had only one mitten, so back he went to see where he might have dropped the other one. But all he could find were the ripped-apart pieces. And he thought he saw a little mouse scurrying away with a bit of red wool perched on her head.

It looked very much like the lining from the thumb of his missing mitten.

"Oh, well," said the boy as he snuggled his cold hand inside his coat, "my grandmother will surely have my new mittens finished by now."

Then he hurried home, with the north wind nipping at his cheeks.

And my grandfather says he never did know what *really* happened to his mitten.

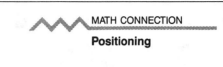
Hokey Pokey

Letting children act out the Hokey Pokey makes learning about right *and* left *more fun.*

With a swing   *American Singing Game*

1. You put your right foot in, You put your
2. You put your left foot in, You put your

right foot out, You put your right foot in and you
left foot out, You put your left foot in and you

shake it all a-bout; You do the Ho - key Po - key and you
shake it all a-bout; You do the Ho - key Po - key and you

turn your-self a-round. That's what it's all a - bout!
turn your-self a-round. That's what it's all a - bout!

3. You put your right arm in . . .

4. You put your left arm in . . .

5. You put your whole self in . . .

Use with Grade K, Chapter 2, Lesson 1

Read-Aloud Selections
Grade K, Side 1, Selection 2

MATH CONNECTIONS

Classifying
Positioning
Money

Caps For Sale

BY ESPHYR SLOBODKINA

A peddler who sells hats keeps track of his wares by sorting them by color. This story also lends itself to discussion of positional terms and money.

Once there was a peddler who sold caps. But he was not like an ordinary peddler carrying his wares on his back. He carried them on top of his head.

First he had on his own checked cap, then a bunch of gray caps, then a bunch of brown caps, then a bunch of blue caps, and on the very top a bunch of red caps.

He walked up and down the streets, holding himself very straight so as not to upset his caps.

As he went along he called, "Caps! Caps for sale! Fifty cents a cap!"

One morning he couldn't sell any caps. He walked up the street and he walked down the street calling, "Caps! Caps for sale. Fifty cents a cap."

But nobody wanted any caps that morning. Nobody wanted even a red cap.

He began to feel very hungry, but he had no money for lunch.

"I think I'll go for a walk in the country," said he. And he walked out of town—slowly, slowly, so as not to upset his caps.

He walked for a long time until he came to a great big tree.

"That's a nice place for a rest," thought he.

And he sat down very slowly under the tree and leaned back little by little against the tree-trunk so as not to disturb the caps on his head.

Then he put up his hand to feel if they were straight—first his own checked cap, then the gray caps, then the brown caps, then the blue caps, then the red caps on the very top.

They were all there.

So he went to sleep.

He slept for a long time.

When he woke up he was refreshed and rested.

But before standing up he felt with his hand to make sure his caps were in the right place.

All he felt was his own checked cap!

He looked to the right of him.

No caps.

He looked to the left of him.

No caps.

He looked to the back of him.

No caps.

He looked behind the tree.

No caps.

Then he looked up into the tree.

And what do you think he saw?

On every branch sat a monkey. On every monkey was a gray, or a brown, or a blue, or a red cap!

The peddler looked at the monkeys.

The monkeys looked at the peddler.

He didn't know what to do.

Finally he spoke to them.

"You monkeys, you," he said, shaking a finger at them, "you give me back my caps."

But the monkeys only shook their fingers back at him and said, "Tsz, tsz, tsz."

This made the peddler angry, so he shook both hands at them and said, "You monkeys, you! You give me back my caps."

But the monkeys only shook both their hands back at him and said, "Tsz, tsz, tsz."

Now he felt quite angry. He stamped his foot, and he said, "You monkeys, you! You better give me back my caps!"

But the monkeys only stamped their feet back at him and said, "Tsz, tsz, tsz."

By this time the peddler was really very, very angry. He stamped both his feet and shouted, "You monkeys, you! You must give me back my caps!"

But the monkeys only stamped both their feet back at him and said, "Tsz, tsz, tsz."

At last he became so angry that he pulled off his own cap, threw it on the ground, and began to walk away.

But then, each monkey pulled off his cap. . .

and all the gray caps,

and all the brown caps,

and all the blue caps,

and all the red caps came flying down out of the tree.

So the peddler picked up his caps and put them back on his head—

first his own checked cap,

then the gray caps,

then the brown caps,

then the blue caps,

then the red caps on the very top.

And slowly, slowly, he walked back to town calling, "Caps! Caps for sale! Fifty cents a cap!"

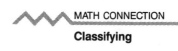
There are Big Waves

BY ELEANOR FARJEON

Eleanor Farjeon's poem shows how waves can be sorted—by color, by size, and by sound.

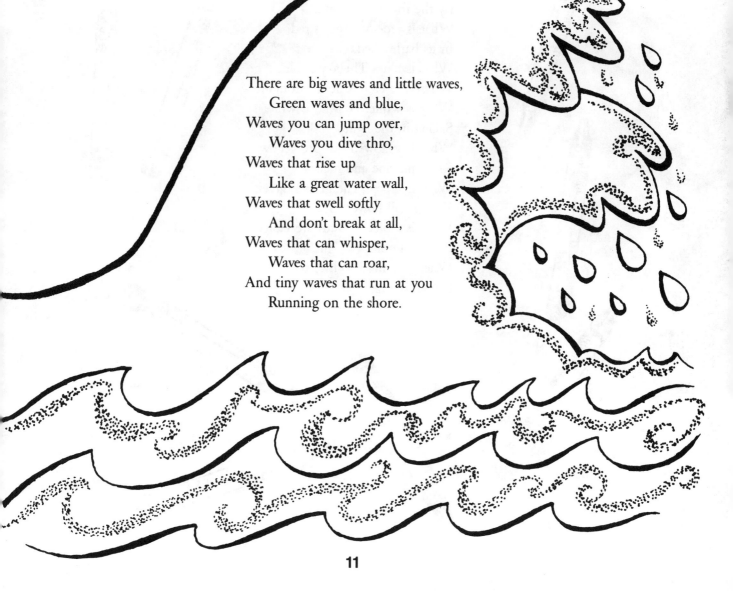

There are big waves and little waves,
　　Green waves and blue,
Waves you can jump over,
　　Waves you dive thro',
Waves that rise up
　　Like a great water wall,
Waves that swell softly
　　And don't break at all,
Waves that can whisper,
　　Waves that can roar,
And tiny waves that run at you
　　Running on the shore.

11

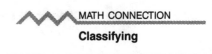
What Is Pink?

BY CHRISTINA ROSSETTI

This poem explores classifying objects by color.

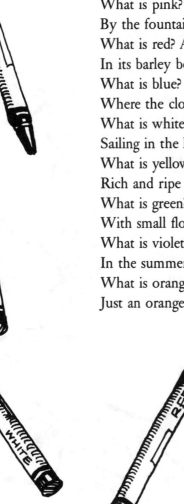

What is pink? A rose is pink
By the fountain's brink.
What is red? A poppy's red
In its barley bed.
What is blue? The sky is blue
Where the clouds float through.
What is white? A swan is white
Sailing in the light.
What is yellow? Pears are yellow,
Rich and ripe and mellow.
What is green? The grass is green,
With small flowers between.
What is violet? Clouds are violet
In the summer twilight,
What is orange? Why, an orange,
Just an orange!

Use with Grade K, Chapter 2, Lesson 4
Grade K, Chapter 2, Lesson 5

Math Songs
Side 1, Selection 3

MATH CONNECTIONS

Classifying
Patterning

Hello Song

The words of the "Hello Song" provide an excellent sorting activity in which children sort themselves by the color of their clothes.

Traditional

Hel - lo, hel - lo, How do you do? How do you do?

How do you do? Hel - lo, hel - lo, How do you do?

How do you do to - day? If you're wear - ing { 1. yel - low, 2. green____ 3. red____ }

stand up. If you're wear - ing { 1. yel - low, 2. green____ 3. red____ } stand up.

(slower beat)

1. Pat, pat, pat your legs, Pat, pat, pat your legs,
2. Stamp, stamp, stamp your feet, Stamp, stamp, stamp your feet,
3. Nod, nod, nod your head, Nod, nod, nod your head,

Pat, pat, pat your legs, Pat your legs to - day.
Stamp, stamp, stamp your feet, Stamp your feet to - day.
Nod, nod, nod your head, Nod your head to - day.

Use with Grade K, Chapter 3, Lesson 1
Grade K, Chapter 3, Lesson 2

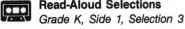 **Read-Aloud Selections**
Grade K, Side 1, Selection 3

MATH CONNECTIONS
Patterning
Counting
Adding
Subtracting

Too Much Noise

BY ANN McGOVERN

Children can listen to the tape and then repeat the sounds that kept Peter awake. The story also offers examples of more *and* fewer, *which can be expanded to explore counting to 10 and addition and subtraction.*

$\mathcal{A}$ long time ago there was an old man.
His name was Peter, and he lived in an old, old house.

The bed creaked.
The floor squeaked.
Outside, the wind blew the leaves through the trees.
The leaves fell on the roof. *Swish. Swish.*
The tea kettle whistled. *Hiss. Hiss.*
"Too noisy," said Peter.

Peter went to see the wise man of the village.
"What can I do?" Peter asked the wise man.
"My house makes too much noise.
My bed creaks.
My floor squeaks.
The wind blows the leaves through the trees.
The leaves fall on the roof. *Swish. Swish.*
My tea kettle whistles. *Hiss. Hiss.*"

"I can help you," the wise man said. "I know
what you can do."
"What?" said Peter.
"Get a cow," said the wise man.

14

"What good is a cow?" said Peter.
But Peter got a cow anyhow.

The cow said, "Moo. MOO."
The bed creaked.
The floor squeaked.
The leaves fell on the roof. *Swish. Swish.*
The tea kettle whistled. *Hiss. Hiss.*

"Too noisy," said Peter.
And he went back to the wise man.
"Get a donkey," said the wise man.
"What good is a donkey?" said Peter.
But Peter got a donkey anyhow.

The donkey said, "HEE-Haw."
The cow said, "Moo. MOO."
The bed creaked.
The floor squeaked.
The leaves fell on the roof. *Swish. Swish.*
The tea kettle whistled. *Hiss. Hiss.*

"Still too noisy," said Peter.
And he went back to the wise man.

"Get a sheep," said the wise man.
"What good is a sheep?" said Peter.
But Peter got a sheep anyhow.

The sheep said, "Baa. Baa."
The donkey said, "HEE-Haw."
The cow said, "Moo. MOO."
The bed creaked.
The floor squeaked.
The leaves fell on the roof. *Swish. Swish.*
The tea kettle whistled. *Hiss. Hiss.*
"Too noisy," said Peter.
And he went back to the wise man.

"Get a hen," said the wise man.
"What good is a hen?" said Peter.
But Peter got a hen anyhow.

The hen said, "Cluck. Cluck."
The sheep said, "Baa. Baa."
The donkey said, "HEE-Haw."
The cow said, "Moo. MOO."
The bed creaked.
The floor squeaked.
The leaves fell on the roof. *Swish. Swish.*
The tea kettle whistled. *Hiss. Hiss.*

"Too noisy," said Peter.
And back he went to the wise man.

"Get a dog," the wise man said.
"And get a cat too."
"What good is a dog?" said Peter.
"Or a cat?"
But Peter got a dog and a cat anyhow.

The dog said, "Woof. Woof."
The cat said, "Mee-ow. Mee-ow."
The hen said, "Cluck. Cluck."
The sheep said, "Baa. Baa."
The donkey said, "HEE-Haw."
The cow said, "Moo. MOO."
The bed creaked.
The floor squeaked.
The leaves fell on the roof. *Swish. Swish.*
The tea kettle whistled. *Hiss. Hiss.*

Now Peter was angry.
He went to the wise man.

"I told you my house was too noisy," he said.
"I told you my bed creaks.
My floor squeaks.
The leaves fall on the roof. *Swish. Swish.*
The tea kettle whistles. *Hiss. Hiss.*
You told me to get a cow.
All day the cow says, 'Moo. MOO.'
You told me to get a donkey.
All day the donkey says, 'HEE-Haw.'
You told me to get a sheep.
All day the sheep says, 'Baa. Baa.'
You told me to get a hen.
All day the hen says, 'Cluck. Cluck.'
You told me to get a dog.
And a cat.
All day the dog says, 'Woof, Woof.'
All day the cat says, 'Mee-ow. Mee-ow.'
I am going crazy," said Peter.

The wise man said, "Do what I tell you.
Let the cow go.
Let the donkey go.
Let the sheep go.
Let the hen go.
Let the dog go.
Let the cat go."

So Peter let the cow go.
He let the donkey go.
He let the sheep go.
He let the hen go.
He let the dog go.
He let the cat go.

Now no cow said, "Moo. MOO."
No donkey said, "HEE-Haw."
No sheep said, "Baa. Baa."
No hen said, "Cluck. Cluck."
No dog said, "Woof. Woof."
No cat said, "Mee-ow. Mee-ow."

The bed creaked.
"Ah," said Peter. "What a quiet noise."

The floor squeaked.
"Oh," said Peter. "What a quiet noise."

Outside the leaves fell on the roof. *Swish. Swish.*
Inside the tea kettle whistled. *Hiss. Hiss.*
"Ah. Oh," said Peter. "How quiet my house is."

And Peter got into his bed and went to sleep
and dreamed a very quiet dream.

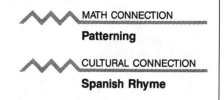
Little Fish

SELECTED AND TRANSLATED BY MARGOT C. GRIEGO, BETSY L. BUCKS, SHARON S. GILBERT AND LAUREL H. KIMBALL

This is a translation of a Spanish rhyme. Children may enjoy extending the pattern for the motions of the little fish and making their own finger plays, or creating a pattern for another animal.

Little fish move in the water, swim, swim, swim.
  (Swimming motion with hands.)
Fly, fly, fly.
  (Flap arms.)
Little ones, little ones.
  (Thumb and fingers together.)
Fly, fly, fly.
  (Repeat actions.)
Swim, swim, swim.

If You're Happy

The last verse of this song asks children to create a pattern by putting together the movements of the three previous verses.

Traditional

1. If you're hap-py and you know it, clap your hands.

If you're hap-py and you know it, clap your hands.

If you're hap-py and you know it,

Then your face will sure-ly show it.

If you're hap-py and you know it, clap your hands.

2. If you're happy and you know it, tap your foot.

3. If you're happy and you know it, nod your head.

4. If you're happy and you know it, do all three.

20

Use with Grade K, Chapter 4, Lesson 1

 Read-Aloud Selections
Grade K, Side 1, Selection 4

MATH CONNECTIONS

Counting
Adding
Subtracting

Hattie and the Fox

BY MEM FOX

The 5 animals in Hattie's chorus, and the various parts of the fox, can help children understand the numbers 0 to 5.

Hattie was a big black hen.
One morning she looked up and said,
"Goodness gracious me!
I can see a nose in the bushes!"

"Good grief!" said the goose.
"Well, well!" said the pig.
"Who cares?" said the sheep.
"So what?" said the horse.
"What next?" said the cow.

And Hattie said,
"Goodness gracious me!
I can see a nose and two eyes in the bushes!"

"Good grief!" said the goose.
"Well, well!" said the pig.
"Who cares?" said the sheep.
"So what?" said the horse.
"What next?" said the cow.

And Hattie said,
"Goodness gracious me!
I can see a nose, two eyes, and two ears in
the bushes!"

"Good grief!" said the goose.
"Well, well!" said the pig.
"Who cares?" said the sheep.
"So what?" said the horse.
"What next?" said the cow.

And Hattie said,
"Goodness gracious me!
I can see a nose, two eyes, two ears, and two
legs in the bushes!"

"Good grief!" said the goose.
"Well, well!" said the pig.
"Who cares?" said the sheep.
"So what?" said the horse.
"What next?" said the cow.

And Hattie said,
"Goodness gracious me!
I can see a nose, two eyes, two ears, two legs,
and a body in the bushes!"

"Good grief!" said the goose.
"Well, well!" said the pig.
"Who cares?" said the sheep.
"So what?" said the horse.
"What next?" said the cow.

And Hattie said,
"Goodness gracious me!
I can see a nose, two eyes, two ears, a body,
four legs, and a tail in the bushes! It's a fox!
It's a fox!"
And she flew very quickly into a nearby tree.

"Oh, no!" said the goose.
"Dear me!" said the pig.
"Oh, dear!" said the sheep.
"Oh, help!" said the horse.
But the cow said, "MOO!"
so loudly that the fox was frightened and
ran away.

And they were all so surprised that none of
them said anything for a very long time.

Use with Grade K, Chapter 4, Lesson 3
Grade K, Chapter 4, Lesson 5

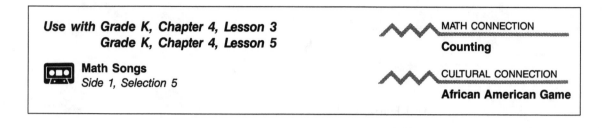

Math Songs
Side 1, Selection 5

MATH CONNECTION
Counting

CULTURAL CONNECTION
African American Game

Draw a Bucket of Water

The numbers 1 to 4 are highlighted in this song, which is an African American play party game.

African American Play Party Game

Draw   a   buck - et   of   wa -   ter

for   my   on - ly   daugh -   ter.

One   rack - a - shack - a - shack - a,   Two   rack - a - shack - a - shack - a,

Three   rack - a - shack - a - shack - a,   Four   rack - a - shack - a - shack - a.

Let   this   old   { la - dy / man ___ }   un - der ___

Let this old {la - dy / man___} un - der. ___

Four in the sug - ar bowl, hop! hop! hop!

Four in the sug - ar bowl, hop! hop! hop!

Use with Grade K, Chapter 5, Lesson 1

Read-Aloud Selections
Grade K, Side 1, Selection 5

MATH CONNECTIONS
Comparing
Measuring
Geometry
Adding

Couldn't We Have a Turtle Instead?

BY JUDITH VIGNA

Can 11 different kinds of animals fit inside a little girl's room? The variety of animals here offers opportunities for comparing and measuring, studying geometric shapes, and exploring addition.

"We're going to have a baby,"
Lizzie's mother said.

"A little brother or sister for Lizzie.
The baby will share your room,
and we'll move out your toy box—
to make a place for the crib."

"I don't think there's room
for a baby," Lizzie said.
"Couldn't we have a turtle instead?
He'd sleep in a little box under my bed.

"I'd much rather have a hamster or guppy—
they'd take up less room than even a puppy.

"Couldn't we have a little gray cat?
All she would need is a little round mat.
She'd stay in my room and not get in the way.
And if she had kittens, we'd give them away.

"Couldn't we have a donkey instead?
I'd sleep on the rug, and he'd sleep in my bed.

"Or a lion or tiger
or monkey or bear?
I could quite easily
fit them in here.
One on the canopy,
two on the floor,
three in the closet,
four in the drawer.

"Couldn't we have a giraffe—
not too tall?
If he can't fit in here,
he could use half the hall.

"Or even an elephant? Some are just dears
and wouldn't mind having to sleep on the stairs.

"No," said Lizzie. "I don't think there's room for a baby."

"But," said Lizzie's mother.
"Now that you've found all your animals a
place to sleep, who is going to feed and clean
  a turtle
  a hamster
  several guppies
  a cat
  a donkey
  one lion
  two bears
  three tigers
  four monkeys
  a giraffe
  and an elephant that keeps falling down stairs?

"You would be too busy to play with your toys,
and I would be too busy to play with you."

"I think we'd better have a baby," Lizzie said.

Okay Everybody

BY KARLA KUSKIN

All children can relate to Karla Kuskin's fun poem about being smaller and being taller.
You can use it as a basis for comparing and measuring activities.

Okay everybody, listen to this:
I am tired of being smaller
Than you
And them
And him
And trees and buildings.
So watch out
All you gorillas and adults
Beginning tomorrow morning
Boy
Am I going to be taller.

Use with Grade K, Chapter 6, Lesson 1
Grade K, Chapter 6, Lesson 3
Grade K, Chapter 6, Lesson 4

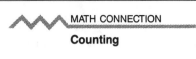
MATH CONNECTION
Counting

Read-Aloud Selections
Grade K, Side 1, Selection 6

Over in the Meadow

TRADITIONAL

This traditional song illustrates the numbers 1 to 12 in the form of animal families, which can be ordered and then compared.

1. Over in the meadow in the sand in the sun,
Lived Old Mother Turtle and her little turtle one.
"Wink," said his mother. "I wink," said the one.
So they winked, and they blinked in the sand in the sun.

2. Over in the meadow where the stream runs through,
Lived Old Mother Fish and her little fishes two.
"Swim," said their mother. "We swim," said the two.
So they swam all day where the stream runs through.

3. Over in the meadow in a hole in a tree,
Lived Old Mother Owl and her little owlets three.
"Hoot," said their mother. "We hoot," said the three.
So they hooted all day in the hole in the tree.

4. Over in the meadow 'neath the old barn floor,
Lived Old Mother Mouse and her little mice four.
"Scamper," said their mother. "We scamper," said the four.
So they scampered all day 'neath the old barn floor.

5. Over in the meadow in a big beehive,
Lived Old Mother Bee and her little bees five,
"Hum," said their mother. "We hum," said the five.
So they hummed all day 'round the big beehive.

29

6. Over in the meadow in a nest built of sticks,
Lived Old Mother Raven and her little ravens six.
"Croak," said their mother. "We croak," said the six.
So they croaked all day in the nest built of sticks.

7. Over in the meadow where the land lies so even,
Lived Old Mother Toad and her little toads seven.
"Hop," said their mother. "We hop," said the seven.
So they hopped all day where the land lies so even.

8. Over in the meadow by an old mossy gate,
Lived Old Mother Possum and her little possums eight.
"Play possum," said their mother. "We play," said the eight.
So they possumed all day by the old mossy gate.

9. Over in the meadow near a loblolly pine,
Lived Old Mother Mole and her little moles nine.
"Burrow," said their mother. "We burrow," said the nine.
So they burrowed all day near the loblolly pine.

10. Over in the meadow in a cozy pig pen,
Lived Old Mother Pig and her little piglets ten.
"Squeal," said their mother. "We squeal," said the ten.
So they squealed all day in their cozy pig pen.

11. Over in the meadow in the soft summer heaven,
Lived Old Mother Firefly and her little flies eleven.
"Shine," said their mother. "We shine," said the eleven.
So they shone like stars in the soft summer heaven.

12. Over in the meadow where the river banks shelve,
Lived Old Mother Beaver and her little beavers twelve.
"Gnaw," said their mother. "We gnaw," said the twelve.
So they gnawed all day where the river banks shelve.

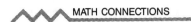
A Counting Rhyme

BY M. M. STEPHENSON

If 3 pigs fall into a tub of tar, 6 pigs go to the moon, and 9 pigs look for gold, how many pigs are there? It depends on how you group them!

One little,
Two little,
Three little pigs,
Small and fat and pink,
Fell into a tub of tar
And turned as black as ink.
Four little,
Five little,
Six little pigs
Went to see the moon;
They found it colder than they thought,
And came back very soon.
Seven little,
Eight little,
Nine little pigs
Went to look for gold;
They found it in a pickle-jar,
At least, that's what I'm told.

31

Use with Grade K, Chapter 6, Lesson 5

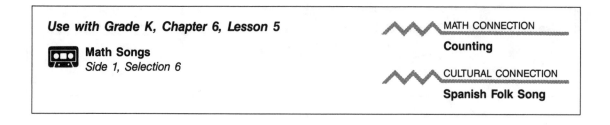

Math Songs
Side 1, Selection 6

MATH CONNECTION
Counting

CULTURAL CONNECTION
Spanish Folk Song

Hurry, Little Pony

Listening to this Spanish folk song will acquaint children with the numbers 1 to 8. You may want to help children create a finger play to act out the numbers in both languages.

Spanish Folk Song
Words by S.S.

1. Hur - ry, lit - tle po - ny, to the town we go.
2. Hur - ry lit - tle po - ny, back to home we go.
3. ¡Ar - ré ca - ba - lli - to! Va - mos a Be - lén

Hur - ry lit - tle po - ny, not too fast or slow.
Hur - ry, lit - tle po - ny, not too fast or slow.
Que ma - ña - na es fi - e - sta y pa - sa - do tam - bi - én.

Ⓑ *(for verses 1 and 2)*

One, two, three, four, five, six, sev-en eight
Po - ny, po - ny, you are great!

Ⓑ *(for verse 3)*

U - no, dos, tres, cua - tro cin - co, seis, si - e - te, o - cho.

Ar - ré ca - ba - lli - to Us - ted me gus - ta mu - cho.

Use with Grade K, Chapter 7, Lesson 1

 Read-Aloud Selections
Grade K, Side 2, Selection 1

〰〰〰 MATH CONNECTIONS
Geometry
Fractions

Tatum's Favorite Shape

BY DOROTHY THOLE

Tatum's mother helps him discover and name geometric shapes in his own house and yard. She also teaches her son about the meaning of one half. This story can encourage children and parents to see their own surroundings in a new way.

Mama heard the school bus stopping at the corner. The screen door slammed and Tatum stomped into the kitchen

"Mama, I'm not going to school tomorrow," he said. "I'm not ever going back."

Mama reached over and took Tatum's baseball cap and said, "What is it, son, did you get into a fuss?"

Tatum hung his head down. "No, Mama, I didn't get into a fuss, but I'm not going back to that place again."

"Why, Tatum, you told me yesterday that you had three stars on your chart."

"I do, Mama. One for tying my shoes, one for knowing my colors, and one for counting to one hundred."

Mama said, "Seems to me you're doing fine. Why aren't you happy?"

"Today we could get a star for knowing our shapes and, Mama, I got them all mixed up."

"Tatum, your mama is going to play a game with you and I'll bet you get a star on your chart tomorrow."

"Can we play it right now?"

"Uh-huh," said Mama. "I'll just put Sissy in her high chair."

Tatum giggled. "What do I do, Mama? Do I need a piece of paper?"

"You just come with me, son."

Mama took Tatum's hand and they went into the bedroom.

"Now, let's play," said Mama. "Close your eyes."

Tatum squeezed his eyes shut and yelled, "I'm ready!"

Mama put her hand on top of his head. "Don't yell so loud, honey. Your eyes are shut, but my ears are open."

She picked up one of Tatum's blocks and put it in his hands. "What shape is it?" she asked.

Tatum felt the corners and sides. "I know it's one of my blocks," he said, "but it mixes me up. Is it a square or one of those rectangles?"

"Let's find out," Mama said. "Put your hands on my waist and follow me like a train."

Mama led Tatum to the other bedroom. She reached down and handed him a shoe box. "Is this a square?" she said.

Tatum felt the long top and answered, "No, Mama, that's a rectangle so the block *was* a square. Am I right, Mama? Am I right?"

"Right," said Mama. "Now keep your eyes closed and let's make the train again."

Mama led Tatum out into the yard.

"All right," said Mama. "Open your eyes and tell me what you see."

"My swing!" said Tatum.

"Uh-huh," said Mama. "Can you tell me what shape it is?"

"A circle!" Tatum yelled.

"You sure are smart," said Mama. "Come on, I'll give you a swing, and you tell me the shapes you've learned. Can you remember?"

"Uh-huh," said Tatum. "The block was a square, the shoe box was a rectangle, and my swing is a circle. There's another shape I have to learn, Mama, but I don't remember what it is."

"Let's go have some lunch and then I'll help you to remember."

Tatum sat down at the kitchen table. Mama fixed him a bowl of chicken noodle soup. Then she fixed him a sandwich and a glass of milk.

"See this sandwich?" she said. "What shape is it?"

"I know, Mama. It's a square," Tatum said.

"Uh-huh," said Mama, "but watch what I do."

Mama cut the sandwich in half. "Now what shape is this half-a-sandwich?" she asked.

"I remember now, Mama. Three points—it's a triangle!"

"You will know tomorrow when Miss Powell asks you, won't you Tatum?"

"Yes, Mama, but..."

"But what?" said Mama.

"Are those all the shapes there are in the world?" asked Tatum.

Mama said, "No, dear, everything has its own shape."

"Then Miss Powell won't know my favorite shape," Tatum said, "It's not a circle or a square, or a rectangle, or a triangle."

Mama said, "I'll bet I know. It's a star shape."

"No, Mama," said Tatum, "my favorite shape is...YOU!"

Square as a House

BY KARLA KUSKIN

What would it be like to be as square as a house? Children will love pretending to be other shapes and making up their own poems. The colors in the poem can be a source for activities that focus on classifying.

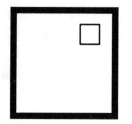

What would you choose
If you were free
To be anything fat
That you wanted to be?
Anything thin or long or tall,
Anything red, blue, black, at all;
A bird on the wing
Or a fish on the fin?
If you're ready to choose
It is time to begin.

If you could be square
Would you be a box
Containing a cake
Or a house
Or blocks
With painted letters
From A to Z?
Who would you
Which would you
What would you be?

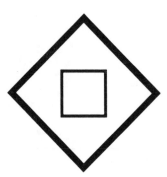

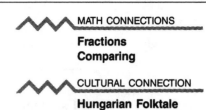

MATH CONNECTIONS

Fractions
Comparing

CULTURAL CONNECTION

Hungarian Folktale

Two Greedy Bears

BY MIRRA GINSBURG

Mirra Ginsburg has adapted this story from a Hungarian folktale. She tells how two bears—with the help of a sly fox—divide a piece of cheese into 2 equal parts.

Two bear cubs went out to see the world.

They walked and walked, till they came to a brook.

"I'm thirsty," said one.
"I'm thirstier," said the other.

They put their heads down to the water and drank.

"You had more," cried one, and drank some more.
"Now you had more," cried the other, and drank some more.

And so they drank and drank, and their stomachs got bigger and bigger, till a frog peeked out of the water and laughed.

"Look at those pot-bellied bear cubs! If they drink any more they'll burst!"

The bear cubs sat down on the grass and looked at their stomachs.

"I have a stomach ache," one cried.
"I have a bigger one," cried the other.
They cried and cried, till they fell asleep.

In the morning they woke up feeling better
and continued their journey.

"I am hungry," said one.
"I am hungrier," said the other.

And suddenly they saw a big round cheese lying
by the roadside. They wanted to divide it.
But they did not know how to break it into
equal parts. Each was afraid the other would
get the bigger piece.

They argued, and they growled, and they began
to fight, till a fox came by.

"What are you arguing about?" the sly one asked
the bear cubs.
"We don't know how to divide the cheese so that
we'll both get equal parts."
"That's easy," she said. "I'll help you."

She took the cheese and broke it in two.
But she made sure that one piece was bigger
than the other, and the bear cubs cried,
"That one is bigger!"

"Don't worry. I know what to do." And she
took a big bite out of the larger piece.
"Now that one's bigger!"

"Have patience!" And she
took a bite out of the second piece.
"Now this one's bigger!"

"Wait, wait," the fox said with her mouth full
of cheese. "In just a moment they'll be equal."
She took another bite, and then another.

38

And the bear cubs kept turning their black noses
from the bigger piece to the smaller one,
from the smaller one to the bigger one.
"Now this one's bigger!"
"Now that one's bigger!"

And the fox kept on dividing and dividing the cheese,
till she could eat no more. "And now, good appetite
to you, my friends!" She flicked her tail and
stalked away.

By then all that was left of the big round
cheese were two tiny crumbs.
But they were equal!

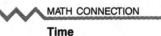
Jesse Bear, What Will You Wear?

BY NANCY WHITE CARLSTROM

The sequence of morning, noon, and night is developed as Jesse Bear decides which clothes are appropriate for the time of day.

Jesse Bear, what will you wear?
What will you wear in the morning?

My shirt of red
Pulled over my head
Over my head in the morning.

I'll wear my pants
My pants that dance
My pants that dance in the morning.

I'll wear a rose
Between my toes
A rose in my toes in the morning.

I'll wear the sun
On my legs that run
Sun on the run in the morning.

I'll wear the sand
On my arm and hand
Sand on my hand in the morning.

Jesse Bear, what will you wear
What will you wear at noon?

I'll wear my chair.

You'll wear your chair?

I'll wear my chair
Because I'm stuck there
Stuck in my chair at noon.

I'll wear carrots and peas
And a little more please

Celery crunch
And sprouts in a bunch

An apple to bite
And a moustache of white

Juice from a pear
And rice in my hair
That's what I'll wear at noon.

Jesse Bear, what will you wear
What will you wear at night?

Not my shirt
It's covered with dirt
Not my pants
That sat in the ants
Ants in my pants tonight.

Jesse Bear, what will you wear
What will you wear at night?

Water to float
My bubbles and boat
I'll wear in the tub tonight.

My pj's with feet
And face on the seat

My blanket that's blue
And plays peek-a-boo

Bear hugs from you
And three kisses too
That's what I'll wear tonight.

Jesse Bear, what will you wear
What will you wear at night?

Sleep in my eyes
And stars in the skies
Moon on my bed
And dreams in my head
That's what I'll wear tonight.

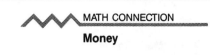
Money's Funny

BY MARY ANN HOBERMAN

As Mary Ann Hoberman points out, if it were a matter of size, a penny would be worth more than a dime.

Money's funny
Don't you think?
Nickel's bigger than a dime;
So's a cent;
But when they're spent,
Dime is worth more
Every time.

Money's funny.

43

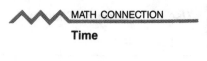
Peanut Butter

There's more to making a sandwich than spreading peanut butter and jelly on a piece of bread. What sequence of events has to happen before that? You have to dig the peanuts and pick the grapes and then squish them.

Camp Song

Refrain

Swing G6 (whisper) Fine

Pea - nut,___ pea - nut but - ter___ jel - ly.

Verse *(spoken)*

G6

1. *First*   *you*   *dig*   *some pea* - *nuts,*
2. *Then*   *you*   *pick*   *some grapes,*___
3. *Then*   *you*   *take*   *some bread,*___

G6

and   *you*   *dig*   *'em,*   *you*   *dig*   *'em,*
and   *you*   *pick*   *'em,*   *you*   *pick*   *'em,*
and   *you spread*   *it,*   *you spread*   *it,*

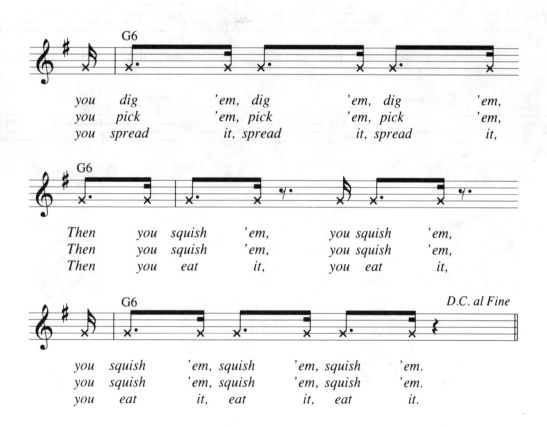

you   dig   'em, dig   'em, dig   'em,
you   pick   'em, pick   'em, pick   'em,
you   spread   it, spread   it, spread   it,

Then   you   squish   'em,   you squish   'em,
Then   you   squish   'em,   you squish   'em,
Then   you   eat   it,   you eat   it,

D.C. al Fine

you   squish   'em, squish   'em, squish   'em.
you   squish   'em, squish   'em, squish   'em.
you   eat   it, eat   it, eat   it.

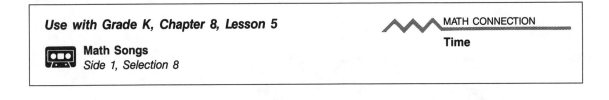
Who Has the Penny?

Let children rewrite this traditional song by using a variety of coins.

Traditional

do

Who   has   the   pen - ny?   (I   have   the   pen - ny.)

Who   has   the   pin?   (I   have   the   pin.)

Use with Grade K, Chapter 9, Lesson 1

 Read-Aloud Selections
Grade K, Side 2, Selection 3

MATH CONNECTIONS
Adding
Subtracting

Annie's Pet

BY BARBARA BRENNER

Annie has 5 dollars to buy a pet, but each time she stops, she ends up with 1 dollar less.
Can she get a pet for 0 dollars?

On her birthday, Annie went to the zoo. That's where she got a great idea. "I have five birthday dollars," she said to her family. "I'm going to buy an animal."

Annie didn't know what kind of animal she wanted. But she knew what she didn't want.

"I don't want a bear," she said. "Bears are too hairy. I don't want a snake. You can't take a snake for a walk."

"Try not to buy too big an animal," said her father.

"You don't want too small an animal," said her mother.

"Get a wild animal," said her brother.

"I don't want a wild animal," said Annie. "I want a *pet.*"

The next day, Annie put on her hat and her backpack. "So long, everybody," she said. "I'm going to buy my pet."

Annie walked down the street until she came to a house. There was a girl with a bird in front of the house. The bird gave Annie an idea.

Annie called to the girl, "Will you sell that bird for five dollars?"

"Not for a million dollars. I love this bird."

"But I need a pet to love, too," said Annie.

"Try the pet store," said the little girl. And she went inside with her bird.

Annie walked a little more. She came to a toy store. The store gave her an idea.

"Do you have toys for pets?" she asked the man inside.

"All kinds," said the man. "Swings, rings, bells, balls."

"I'll take a ball."

"That will be one dollar," said the man. Annie gave the man one dollar. She still had four dollars.

47

Annie walked a little more. She came to a gift shop. A pretty tan cat was sitting in the window.

Annie went into the shop. "How much is that cat in the window?" she asked the woman.

"That cat is not for sale," said the woman. "We do not sell pets. But we do sell pet collars."

"Now that is a great idea," said Annie. "A collar—not too big, not too small." Annie bought a collar for one dollar. She still had three dollars.

Annie walked a little more. She went into a shopping mall. She saw a nice red pet dish and a nice red pet leash. They each cost one dollar. Annie bought the dish and the leash.

"Now I have all the things I'll need for my pet," she said.

Annie's long walk had made her very hungry. She stopped to buy a little snack. It only cost one dollar.

At last, Annie came to the pet store. She looked in the window. There were pets of every size and kind.

"This is it!" cried Annie. "This is where I'll buy my pet." Annie reached into the backpack to get her money. But the money was gone!

She thought about what she had spent—one dollar for a toy...one dollar for a collar...one dollar for a dish...one dollar for a leash...and one dollar for a double-dip cone! Five—Annie had spent all five birthday dollars!

Annie sat down on a stone step to have a good cry. But then she looked up and saw a sign that read: GIVE A PET A HOME.

That's when Annie got the greatest idea of all! She jumped up and ran inside.

"I'm looking for a pet," said Annie.

"Can you give a pet a good home?" asked the woman behind the desk.

"Yes," said Annie. "I have a collar, a toy, a dish, and a leash for my pet. But I don't have any money."

"Do you have love?" asked the woman.

"Oh, yes, I have a lot of that," said Annie.

"Then I have just the pet for you," the woman said.

And she did.

Three Little Monkeys

TRADITIONAL

Three little monkeys are jumping on a bed, but one by one, they fall off!

Three little monkeys jumping on the bed,
One fell off and banged her head.
Mommy called the doctor and the doctor said,
"No more monkeys jumping on the bed!"

Two little monkeys jumping on the bed,
One fell off and banged her head.
Mommy called the doctor and the doctor said,
"No more monkeys jumping on the bed!"

One little monkey jumping on the bed,
One fell off and banged her head.
Mommy called the doctor and the doctor said,
"No more monkeys jumping on the bed!"

Use with Grade K, Chapter 10, Lesson 1

 Read-Aloud Selections
Grade K, Side 2, Selection 4

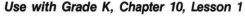 MATH CONNECTIONS

Number Sense
Counting
Time

Moira's Birthday

BY ROBERT MUNSCH

Moira's parents tell her that she can invite 6 kids to her birthday party, but she invites 200! What would happen if your children invited grade 1, grade 2, grade 3, grade 4, grade 5, grade 6, aaaaand kindergarten to a party?

One day, Moira went to her mother and said, "For my birthday I want to invite grade 1, grade 2, grade 3, grade 4, grade 5, grade 6, aaaaand kindergarten."

Her mother said, "Are you crazy? That's too many kids!"

So Moira went to her father and said, "For my birthday I want to invite grade 1, grade 2, grade 3, grade 4, grade 5, grade 6, aaaaand kindergarten."

Her father said, "Are you crazy? That's too many kids. For your birthday you can invite six kids, just six: 1-2-3-4-5-6; and NNNNNO kindergarten!"

So Moira went to school and invited six kids, but a friend who had not been invited came up and said, "Oh Moira, couldn't I please, PLEASE, PLEEEASE COME TO YOUR BIRTHDAY PARTY?"

Moira said, "Ummmmmm...O.K."

By the end of the day Moira had invited grade 1, grade 2, grade 3, grade 4, grade 5, grade 6, aaaaand kindergarten. But she didn't tell her mother and father. She was afraid they might get upset.

On the day of the party someone knocked at the door: rap, rap, rap, rap, rap, rap. Moira opened it and saw six kids. Her father said, "That's it, six kids. Now we can start the party."

Moira said, "Well, let's wait just one minute."

So they waited one minute and something knocked on the door like this: BLAM, BLAM, BLAM, BLAM.

The father and mother opened the door and they saw grade 1, grade 2, grade 3, grade 4, grade 5, grade 6, aaaaand kindergarten. The kids ran in right over the father and mother.

When the father and mother got up off the floor they saw: kids in the basement, kids in the living room, kids in the kitchen, kids in the bedrooms, kids in the bathroom, and kids on the ROOF!

They said, "Moira, how are we going to feed all these kids?"

Moira said, "Don't worry, I know what to do."

She went to the phone and called a place that made pizzas. She said, "To my house please send two hundred pizzas."

The lady at the restaurant yelled, "TWO HUNDRED PIZZAS! ARE YOU CRAZY? TWO HUNDRED PIZZAS IS TOO MANY PIZZAS."

"Well, that is what I want." said Moira.

"We'll send ten," said the lady. "Just ten, ten is all we can send right now." Then she hung up.

Then Moira called a bakery. She said, "To my house please send two hundred birthday cakes."

The man at the bakery yelled, "TWO HUNDRED BIRTHDAY CAKES! ARE YOU CRAZY? THAT IS TOO MANY BIRTHDAY CAKES."

"Well, that is what I want," said Moira.

"We'll send ten," said the man. "Just ten, ten is all we can send right now." Then he hung up.

So a great big truck came and poured just ten pizzas into Moira's front yard. Another truck came and poured just ten birthday cakes into Moira's front yard. The kids looked at that pile of stuff and they all yelled, "FOOD!"

They opened their mouths as wide as they could and ate up all the pizzas and birthday cakes in just five seconds. Then they all yelled, "MORE FOOD!"

"Uh, oh," said the mother. "We need lots more food or there's not going to be a party at all. Who can get us more food, fast?"

The two hundred kids yelled, "WE WILL!" and ran out the door.

Moira waited one hour, two hours, and three hours.

"They're not coming back," said the mother.

"They're not coming back," said the father.

"Wait and see," said Moira.

Then something knocked at the door like this: BLAM, BLAM, BLAM, BLAM.

The mother and father opened it up and the two hundred kids ran in carrying all sorts of food.

There was fried goat, rolled oats, burnt toast and artichokes; old cheese, baked fleas, boiled bats and beans. There was egg nog, pork sog, simmered soup and hot dogs; jam jars, dinosaurs, chocolate bars and stew.

The 200 kids ate the food in just 10 minutes. When they finished eating, everyone gave Moira their present. Moira looked and saw presents in the bedrooms, presents in the bathroom and presents on the roof.

"Oh-oh," said Moira. "The whole house is full of presents. Even I can't use that many presents."

"And who," asked the father, "is going to clean up the mess?"

"I have an idea," said Moira, and she yelled, "Anybody who helps to clean up gets to take home a present."

The two hundred kids cleaned up the house in just five minutes. Then each kid took a present and went out the door.

"Whew," said the mother. "I'm glad that's over."

"Whew," said the father. "I'm glad that's over."

"Uh-oh," said Moira. "I think I hear a truck." A great big dump truck came and poured one hundred and ninety pizzas into Moira's front yard. The driver said, "Here's the rest of your pizzas." Then another dump truck came and poured one hundred and ninety birthday cakes into Moira's front yard. The driver said, "Here's the rest of your birthday cakes."

"How," said the father, "are we going to get rid of all this food?"

"That's easy," said Moira. "We'll just have to do it again tomorrow and have another birthday party! Let's invite grade 1, grade 2, grade 3, grade 4, grade 5, grade 6, aaaaand kindergarten."

THE END

Too Many Daves

BY DR. SEUSS

Mrs. McCave in Dr. Seuss's poem thinks that 23 Daves is 22 too many. She wishes she had given her sons different names.

Did I ever tell you that Mrs. McCave
Had twenty-three sons and she named them all Dave?
Well, she did. And that wasn't a smart thing to do.
You see, when she wants one and calls out, "Yoo-Hoo!
Come into the house, Dave!" she doesn't get *one*.
All twenty-three Daves of hers come on the run!
This makes things quite difficult at the McCaves'
As you can imagine, with so many Daves.
And often she wishes, that when they were born,
She had named one of them Bodkin Van Horn
And one of them Hoos-Foos. And one of them Snimm.
And one of them Hot-Shot. And one Sunny Jim.
And one of them Shadrack. And one of them Blinkey.
And one of them Stuffy. And one of them Stinkey.
Another one Putt-Putt. Another one Moon Face.
Another one Marvin O'Gravel Balloon Face.
And one of them Ziggy. And one Soggy Muff.
One Buffalo Bill. And one Biffalo Buff.
And one of them Sneepy. And one Weepy Weed.
And one Paris Garters. And one Harris Tweed.
And one of them Sir Michael Carmichael Zutt
And one of them Oliver Boliver Butt
And one of them Zanzibar Buck-Buck McFate...
But she didn't do it. And now it's too late.

53

One, Two, Buckle My Shoe

TRADITIONAL

Children may enjoy updating this Mother Goose rhyme that features the numbers 1 to 20.

One, two, buckle my shoe;

Three, four, open the door;

Five, six, pick up sticks;

Seven, eight, lay them straight;

Nine, ten, a big fat hen;

Eleven, twelve, I hope you're well;

Thirteen, fourteen, draw the curtain;

Fifteen, sixteen, the maid's in the kitchen;

Seventeen, eighteen, she's in waiting;

Nineteen, twenty, my stomach's empty.
Please, ma'am, to give me some dinner.

Use with Grade K, Chapter 10, Lesson 5

Math Songs
Side 1, Selection 9

MATH CONNECTION
Number Sense
Counting

CULTURAL CONNECTION
Canadian Street Rhyme

Going over the Sea

Although the verses of this Canadian street rhyme only contain the numbers 1 to 10, you can encourage children to extend the verse by using higher numbers.

Canadian Street Rhyme

1. When I was one I ate a bun, Go-ing o-ver the sea. I jumped a-board a sail-or-man's ship, And the sail-or-man said to me,

Refrain

"Go - ing o - ver, go - ing un - der, Stand at at - ten - tion like a sol - dier, With a one, two, and three."

2. When I was two I buckled my shoe,
3. When I was three I banged my knee,
4. When I was four I shut the door,
5. When I was five I learned to jive,
6. When I was six I picked up sticks,

7. When I was seven I went to heaven,
8. When I was eight I learned to skate,
9. When I was nine I climbed a vine,
10. When I was ten I caught a hen,

55

GRADE

1

STORIES, POEMS, and SONGS

Use with Grade 1, Chapter 1, Lesson 1

 Read-Aloud Selections
Grade 1, Tape 1
Side 1, Selection 1

MATH CONNECTION

Counting

All of Our Noses Are Here

FROM *ALL OF OUR NOSES ARE HERE AND OTHER NOODLE TALES*
RETOLD BY ALVIN SCHWARTZ

This story emphasizes how important it is to count yourself, and to count yourself only once.

FOREWORD

Most noodles are kind and loving people. But they have very few brains. This book is about a whole family of noodles and the silly things they do. They are Mr. and Mrs. Brown, and their children Sam and Jane, and Grandpa.

The Browns went for a ride in their rowboat. When the sun began to go down, they rowed back to shore.

"Everyone line up," said Mr. Brown. "Let us see if anybody fell out of the boat. One is here. Two are here. Three are here. And four are here."

"But we are five," said Mrs. Brown.

"I think I counted wrong," said Mr. Brown. "I will count again. One is here. Two are here. Three are here. And four are here."

"Only four?" asked Mrs. Brown.

"Yes," said Mr. Brown.

"One of us is missing." Mrs. Brown began to cry. So did the others.

"Why are all of you crying?" a fisherman asked.

"Five of us went rowing," said Mr. Brown. "But only four came back."

"Are you sure?" the fisherman asked.

Mr. Brown counted again. Again he counted only four.

"I know what is wrong," said the fisherman. "You forgot to count yourself."

"I will try again," said Mr. Brown. "One is here. Two are here. Three are here. And four are here. And *five* are here. And SIX are here!"

"But there should be five," said Mrs. Brown.

"No," said Mr. Brown. "Now we are six."

"But I do not see anybody else," said Mrs. Brown.

They looked in the rowboat and under the dock and up in the trees and behind all the bushes, but they did not find anyone.

"Come out! Come out! Whoever you are!" Mr. Brown shouted. The others joined in, but nobody came out.

When the fisherman heard the shouting, he went to see what was wrong.

"Now there are six of us instead of five," said Mr. Brown. "But we cannot find this extra person."

"Are you sure there are six?" the fisherman asked.

Mr. Brown counted again, and again he counted six.

"You are doing it all wrong," said the fisherman. "You counted yourself twice. Let me show you the right way to count. Everybody, get down on your hands and knees. Now stick your noses into the mud and pull them out. Now count the holes your noses made."

Mr. Brown counted. "One is here. Two are here. Three are here. Four are here. And *five* are here. All of our noses are here!" he said. "Now we can go home."

Use with Grade 1, Chapter 1, Lesson 3

Math Songs
Side 1, Selection 10

MATH CONNECTION
Counting

CULTURAL CONNECTION
Mexican Folk Song

Counting Song

The numbers 1 to 10 as they appear in the Spanish language are introduced in this counting song, which is from Mexico. When children are familiar with the song, let them use their fingers to count along.

Mexican Folk Song

U - no, dos y tres,

cua - tro, cin - co, seis, sie - te, o - cho,

nue - ve, y a-hor - a diez.

La la la la la la la la la la la la la la la

la. la la la la la la.

Who Wants One?

BY MARY SERFOZO

Despite offers of various objects in groups of 1 to 10, a child only wants 1. You can use this selection to build counting and writing skills and as a basis for comparing and ordering.

Who wants one?

1 Who wants one?
    Do you want one?
    One butterfly, one raisin bun,
    One rainbow coming with the sun.
    Do you want one?
    YES, I WANT ONE!

2 Well, I like two.
    Now won't two do?
    Two shiny shoes, two kangaroos,
    Two kangaroos in shiny shoes.
    Do you want two?
    NO, I WANT ONE!

3 Perhaps it's three
    you want to see.
    Three clocks, three socks, three locks, three keys,
    Three treetops tossing in the breeze.
    Do you want three?
    NO, I WANT ONE!

4 I know. . .it's four
you're waiting for!
Four goats in boats—just four, no more.
Four bright red boots beside the door.
Do you want four?
NO, I WANT ONE!

5 Or maybe five?
Well, sakes alive!
Five peacocks coming up the drive,
Five black bees buzzing 'round the hive.
Do you want five?
NO, I WANT ONE!

6 Do you pick six?
Look, here is six.
Six sails, six whales, six driftwood sticks,
Six jolly dolphins doing tricks.
Do you want six?
NO, I WANT ONE!

7 Then why not seven,
for heaven's sake?
Seven kites and seven cakes,
And seven swans on sky-blue lakes.
Do you want seven?
NO, I WANT ONE!

8 You might like eight.
I think eight's great.
Eight circus clowns all juggling plates,
Eight teddy bears on roller skates.
Do you want eight?
NO, I WANT ONE!

9 You don't want nine,
when nine's so fine?
Nine bluebirds sitting on a sign,
Nine green umbrellas in a line.
Do you want nine?
NO, I WANT ONE!

10 And now here's ten.
Do you want ten?
Ten speckled eggs from ten brown hens,
Ten pink pigs happy in their pens.
Do you want ten?
NO, I WANT ONE!

Well, now, let's just be sure. . .
We'll go back and count again
all the numbers from one to ten.

1 One
2 Two
3 Three
4 Four
5 Five
6 Six
7 Seven
8 Eight
9 Nine
10 Ten

Tell me again,
now that we're done. . .
Do you want one?
YES, I WANT ONE!

Use with Grade 1, Chapter 1, Lesson 6

Math Songs
Side 1, Selection 11

MATH CONNECTION

Counting

CULTURAL CONNECTION

English Folk Song

This Old Man

Counting songs appear in every language. This English folk song features the numbers 1 to 10.

English folk song

1. This old man, he played one, He played nick-nack on my drum. } With a
2. This old man, he played two, He played nick-nack on my shoe.

nick-nack, pad-dy whack, give a dog a bone, This old man came roll-ing home.

3. This old man, he played three,
   He played nick-nack on my tree.

4. This old man, he played four,
   He played nick-nack on my door.

5. This old man, he played five,
   He played nick-nack on my hive.

6. This old man, he played six,
   He played nick-nack on my sticks.

7. This old man, he played seven,
   He played nick-nack on my oven.

8. This old man, he played eight,
   He played nick-nack on my gate.

9. This old man, he played nine,
   He played nick-nack on my line.

10. This old man, he played ten,
    He played nick-nack on my hen.

63

Use with Grade 1, Chapter 2, Lesson 1

 Read-Aloud Selections
Grade 1, Tape 1
Side 1, Selection 2

MATH CONNECTION
Adding

CULTURAL CONNECTION
Russian Folktale

The Enormous Turnip

RETOLD BY KATHY PARKINSON

*Grandfather Ivan and Grandmother Luba can't pull the enormous turnip out of the ground.
They call Olga, who calls Alyosha, the puppy. It finally takes all of them plus a kitten,
a mouse, and a beetle to harvest the turnip.*

Grandfather Ivan planted a turnip in the garden. It grew and it grew and it
GREW. When the time came to pull it up, the turnip was ENORMOUS!
Grandfather took hold of the stem. He pulled and he pulled and he pulled, but
the turnip would not budge. It was stuck fast.

"Grandmother!" he called. "Come and help me pull our turnip!" Grandmother
Luba ran to help. She wrapped her arms around Grandfather's waist.
Grandmother pulled Grandfather while he tugged on the turnip.

They pulled and they pulled and they pulled, but the enormous turnip did
not budge. It was stuck fast.

Grandmother called to Mother, "Natasha, come and help us pull our turnip!"

Mother ran to hold Grandmother's apron while Grandmother pulled
Grandfather, and Grandfather pulled the turnip with all his might.

They pulled and they pulled and they pulled, but still the turnip did not move.

"Olga! Olga!" called Mother to her daughter. "Come and help us pull our
turnip!"

Little Olga ran as fast as she could. She held on to Mother, while Mother
pulled Grandmother, Grandmother pulled Grandfather, and Grandfather tugged
the turnip with all his might.

They pulled and they pulled and they pulled, but still they could not move it.
The enormous turnip was stuck fast.

"Alyosha! Alyosha!" called Olga to her puppy. "Come and help us pull our
turnip!"

Alyosha barked loudly. He ran and took Olga's dress in his teeth. He pulled little Olga, while Olga pulled Mother, Mother pulled Grandmother, Grandmother pulled Grandfather, and Grandfather pulled the turnip with all his might.

They pulled and they pulled and they pulled, but still the turnip would not budge. It was stuck fast.

Alyosha called to Anya the kitten, "Come and help us pull our turnip!"

"Meow! Meow!" mewed Anya. She took Alyosha's tail in her paws. Anya pulled Alyosha, Alyosha pulled little Olga, Olga pulled Mother, Mother pulled Grandmother, Grandmother pulled Grandfather, while Grandfather tugged and tugged with all his might.

They pulled and they pulled and they pulled, but even now the turnip would not move. It was stuck fast.

Manya the mouse heard all the noise. "Squeak! Squeak!" she cried and ran from her hole. She grasped the fur of Anya the kitten. Manya pulled Anya, Anya pulled Alyosha, Alyosha pulled little Olga, Olga pulled Mother, Mother pulled Grandmother, and they all pulled Grandfather, who huffed and puffed as he tugged with all his might.

They pulled and they pulled and they pulled, but the turnip would not budge. It was stuck just as fast as before.

Now Petya the beetle crawled off a leaf. He took the tail of Manya the mouse. Petya pulled Manya, Manya pulled Anya, Anya pulled Alyosha, Alyosha pulled little Olga, Olga pulled Mother, Mother pulled Grandmother, and they all pulled Grandfather, who tugged and tugged on the enormous turnip.

They pulled, and they pulled, and they PULLED! WHOA-OOMP!

They pulled that enormous turnip right out of the ground!

The turnip landed on Grandfather! He fell on Grandmother, Grandmother fell on Mother, Mother fell on little Olga, Olga fell on Alyosha the puppy, Alyosha fell on Anya the kitten, Anya fell on Manya the mouse, but luckily Petya the beetle ran away before anyone fell on him!

That night they all had an *enormous* turnip dinner, and everyone went right to bed, including Petya the beetle.

"How strong I am!" he thought, and he fell fast asleep.

Use with Grade 1, Chapter 2, Lesson 2

⋀⋀⋀ MATH CONNECTIONS
Adding
Subtracting
Counting

⋀⋀⋀ CULTURAL CONNECTION
Mexican Rhyme

The Graceful Elephant

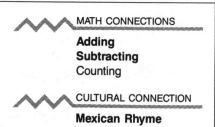

A RHYME FROM MEXICO SELECTED BY LULU DELACRE

How many elephants can balance on a spider's web? In this rhyme from Mexico, an elephant is added with each verse. You may refer children to the "Counting Song" again to increase the number of elephants beyond 5.

One elephant balanced gracefully
Upon a spider's web,
But when the web bounced him all around
He called in another to help hold it down.

Two elephants balanced gracefully
Upon a spider's web,
But when the web bounced them all around
They called in another to help hold it down.

Three elephants balanced gracefully
Upon a spider's web,
But when the web bounced them all around
They called in another to help hold it down.

Four elephants balanced gracefully
Upon a spider's web,
But when the web bounced them all around
They called in another to help hold it down.

Five elephants balanced gracefully
Upon a spider's web,
But when the web bounced them all around
They called in another to help hold it down.

*Un elefante se balanceaba
sobre la tela de una araña,
como veía que resistía
fue a llamar a otro elefante.*

*Dos elefantes se balanceaban
sobre la tela de una araña,
como veían que resistía
fueron a llamar a otro elefante.*

*Tres elefantes se balanceaban
sobre la tela de una araña,
como veían que resistía
fueron a llamar a otro elefante.*

*Cuatro elefantes se balanceaban
sobre la tela de una araña,
como veían que resistía
fueron a llamar a otro elefante.*

*Cinco elefantes se balanceaban
sobre la tela de una araña,
como veían que resistía
fueron a llamar a otro elefante.*

Use with Grade 1, Chapter 2, Lesson 3
Grade 1, Chapter 2, Lesson 4

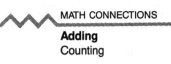

MATH CONNECTIONS

Adding
Counting

Math Songs
Side 2, Selection 1

Johnny Works with One Hammer

Johnny starts work with 1 hammer and accumulates 5 hammers. You can focus on any of the verses to teach addition facts.

American Singing Game

1. John - ny works with one ham - mer,
2. John - ny works with two ham - mers,
3. John - ny works with three ham - mers,
4. John - ny works with four ham - mers,
5. John - ny works with five ham - mers,

one ham - mer, one ham - mer,
two ham - mers, two ham - mers,
three ham - mers, three ham - mers,
four ham - mers, four ham - mers,
five ham - mers, five ham - mers,

John - ny works with one ham - mer,
John - ny works with two ham - mers,
John - ny works with three ham - mers,
John - ny works with four ham - mers,
John - ny works with five ham - mers,

Then he works with two.
Then he works with three.
Then he works with four.
Then he works with five.
Then he works no more.

Use with Grade 1, Chapter 3, Lesson 1

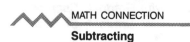
MATH CONNECTION
Subtracting

Read-Aloud Selections
Grade 1, Tape 1
Side 1, Selection 3

Five Little Ducks

A COUNTING SONG BY RAFFI

Every time a mother duck calls her ducklings, 1 less appears. Soon, none appear, but happily, the mother duck finds them all.

Five little ducks went out one day,
Over the hills and far away.
Mother Duck said,
"Quack, quack, quack, quack."
But only four little ducks came back.

Four little ducks went out one day,
Over the hills and far away.
Mother Duck said,
"Quack, quack, quack, quack."
But only three little ducks came back.

Three little ducks went out one day,
Over the hills and far away.
Mother Duck said,
"Quack, quack, quack, quack."
But only two little ducks came back.

Two little ducks went out one day,
Over the hills and far away.
Mother Duck said,
"Quack, quack, quack, quack."
But only one little duck came back.

One little duck went out one day,
Over the hills and far away.
Mother Duck said,
"Quack, quack, quack, quack."
But none of the five little ducks came back.

Sad Mother Duck went out one day,
Over the hills and far away.
Mother Duck said, "Quack, quack, quack, quack."
And all of the five little ducks came back.

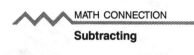
Five Brown Teddies

TRADITIONAL

Keeping track of how many bears are on the wall can help children understand more *and* less *and also counting back to subtract.*

Five brown teddies sitting on a wall,
Five brown teddies sitting on a wall,
And if one brown teddy should accidentally fall,
They'd be four brown teddies sitting on a wall.

Four brown teddies sitting on a wall,
Four brown teddies sitting on a wall,
And if one brown teddy should accidentally fall,
They'd be three brown teddies sitting on a wall.

Three brown teddies sitting on a wall,
Three brown teddies sitting on a wall,
And if one brown teddy should accidentally fall,
They'd be two brown teddies sitting on a wall.

Two brown teddies sitting on a wall,
Two brown teddies sitting on a wall,
And if one brown teddy should accidentally fall,
They'd be one brown teddy sitting on a wall.

One brown teddy sitting on a wall,
One brown teddy sitting on a wall,
And if one brown teddy should accidentally fall,
They'd be no brown teddies sitting there at all!

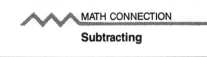
The Cats of Kilkenny

ANONYMOUS

Increasing the number of cats in this poem will produce a variety of subtraction problems with answers of 0 and 1.

There were once two cats of Kilkenny,
Each thought there was one cat too many;
So they fought and they fit,
And they scratched and they bit,
Till, excepting their nails
And the tips of their tails,
Instead of two cats, there weren't any.

There Were Two Wrens

TRADITIONAL

To help children comprehend counting on to add and the meaning of 0, you might let them act out this Mother Goose rhyme.

There were two wrens upon a tree.
Whistle and I'll come to thee.
Another came, and there were three.
Whistle and I'll come to thee.
Another came and there were four.
You needn't whistle anymore.
For being frightened, off they flew.
And there are none to show to you.

Use with Grade 1, Chapter 4, Lesson 1

 Read-Aloud Selections
Grade 1, Tape 1
Side 2, Selection 1

MATH CONNECTIONS
Adding
Subtracting

The Crickets

FROM *MOUSE SOUP* BY ARNOLD LOBEL

If 1 cricket keeps a mouse awake, imagine how disturbing it would be to add 9 more chirping crickets!

One night a mouse woke up. There was a chirping sound outside her window.

"What is that noise?" asked the mouse.

"What did you say?" asked a cricket. "I cannot hear you and make my music at the same time."

"I want to sleep," said the mouse. "I do not want any more music."

"What did you say?" asked the cricket. "You want more music? I will find a friend."

Soon there were two crickets chirping.

"I want you to stop the music," said the mouse. "You are giving me more!"

"What did you say?" asked the cricket. "You want more music? We will find another friend."

Soon there were three crickets chirping.

"You must stop the music," said the mouse. "I am tired. I cannot take much more!"

"What did you say?" asked the cricket. "You want much more music? We will find many friends."

Soon there were ten crickets chirping.

"Stop!" cried the mouse. "Your music is too loud!"

"Loud?" asked the cricket. "Yes, we can chirp loud."

So the ten crickets chirped very loud.

"Please!" shouted the mouse. "I want to sleep. I wish that you would all GO AWAY."

"Go away?" asked the cricket. "Why didn't you say so in the first place?"

"We will go away and chirp somewhere else," said the ten crickets.

They went away and chirped somewhere else. And the mouse went back to sleep.

The Creature in the Classroom

BY JACK PRELUTSKY

How many erasers and notebooks did the creature in Jack Prelutsky's poem devour?
What combinations of 10 objects might the creature eat if it visited your classroom (not
you, we hope!)?

It appeared inside our classroom
at a quarter after ten,
it gobbled up the blackboard,
three erasers and a pen.
It gobbled teacher's apple
and it bopped her with the core.
"How dare you!" she responded.
"You must leave us . . . there's the door."

The Creature didn't listen
but described an arabesque
as it gobbled all her pencils,
seven notebooks and her desk.
Teacher stated very calmly,
"Sir! You simply cannot stay,
I'll report you to the principal
unless you go away."

But the thing continued eating,
it ate paper, swallowed ink,
as it gobbled up our homework
I believe I saw it wink.
Teacher finally lost her temper.
"OUT!" she shouted at the creature.
The creature hopped beside her
and GLOPP. . .it gobbled teacher.

75

Chook, Chook, Chook

TRADITIONAL

Children can explore 3 addends by using Mrs. Hen's chicks as models.

Chook, chook, chook, chook, chook,
Good morning Mrs. Hen.
How many chickens have you got?
Madam, I've got ten.
Four of them are yellow,
And four of them are brown,
And two of them are speckled red,
The nicest in the town.

Use with Grade 1, Chapter 4, Lesson 2

Math Songs
Side 2, Selection 2

MATH CONNECTIONS

Adding
Subtracting
Counting

Ten Little Fingers

To utilize this song in your classroom, you might let pairs of children use their 4 hands to make combinations of 10 fingers.

Traditional

I have ten lit - tle fin - gers and they

all be - long to me! I can make them

do things, Would you like to see?

I can shut them up tight Or o - pen them wide, I can

hold them in front Or make them all hide; I can

hold them up high, I can put them down low; I can

hide them in back, Then hold them just so!

Use with Grade 1, Chapter 5, Lesson 1

Read-Aloud Selections
Grade 1, Tape 1
Side 2, Selection 2

MATH CONNECTIONS

Subtracting
Counting

Ten in a Bed

BY MARY REES

Each of the verses in this traditional song offers a different subtraction problem to model.

There were TEN in the bed
And the little one said,
"Roll over! Roll over!"
So they all rolled over
And one fell out...

There were NINE in the bed
And the little one said,
"Roll over! Roll over!"
So they all rolled over
And one fell out...

There were EIGHT in the bed
And the little one said,
"Roll over! Roll over!"
So they all rolled over
And one fell out...

There were SEVEN in the bed
And the little one said,
"Roll over! Roll over!"
So they all rolled over
And one fell out...

There were SIX in the bed
And the little one said,
"Roll over! Roll over!"
So they all rolled over
And one fell out . . .

There were FIVE in the bed
And the little one said,
"Roll over! Roll over!"
So they all rolled over
And one fell out . . .

There were FOUR in the bed
And the little one said,
"Roll over! Roll over!"
So they all rolled over
And one fell out . . .

There were THREE in the bed
And the little one said,
"Roll over! Roll over!"
So they all rolled over
And one fell out . . .

There were TWO in the bed
And the little one said,
"Roll over! Roll over!"
So they all rolled over
And one fell out . . .

There was ONE in the bed
And the little one said,
"I'm not getting up!"
The other NINE said,
"Oh, yes, you are!"

Then there were NONE in the bed
And no one said,
"Roll over! Roll over!"

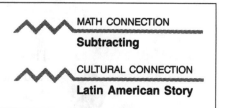

MATH CONNECTION
Subtracting

CULTURAL CONNECTION
Latin American Story

Mexicali Soup

BY KATHRYN HITTE AND WILLIAM D. HAYES

Mama's Mexicali soup is full of wonderful things — peppers, onions, garlic, tomatoes, celery, and potatoes — but what happens when her family asks her to leave out this ingredient and then that one?

*A*ll the way across town Mama sang to herself — to herself and the little one, little Juanita. Here on the streets of the great fine city, she sang an old tune from the old home in the mountains. And she thought of what she would buy in the markets.

Only the best of everything. Potatoes and peppers — the best! Tomatoes and onions — the best! The best garlic. The best celery. And then, cooked all together, ah! The best soup in the world! Mama's Special Mexicali Soup. The soup that always made everyone say, "Mama makes the best soup in the world."

"Ah, *si!*" Mama thought with a smile. "Yes! Our supper tonight will be a very special supper for my Rosie and Antonio and Juan and Manuel and Maria, and for the little one — and for Papa, too. A very special supper of my Mexicali Soup."

"Mama! Yoo-hoo, Mama!"

There was the fine new school building where Juan and Manuel and Maria went to school, and there was Maria with her new city friend, waving and calling.

"Wait a minute, Mama!" Maria came running to put her schoolbooks in the stroller with Juanita.

"Mama, may I play a while at Marjorie's house? Please?"

"Very well," Mama said. "A while. But do not be late for supper, Maria. I am making my special soup tonight."

"Mmmm-mmm, Mexicali Soup!" Maria said. Then she looked thoughtful. Then she frowned. "But — Mama?"

"Yes, Maria?"

"Mama, there is such a lot of potatoes in your Mexicali Soup."

"Of course," Mama said, smiling.

"Marjorie doesn't eat potatoes. Her mother doesn't eat them. Her sister doesn't eat them. Potatoes are too fattening, Mama. They are too fattening for many people in the city. I think we should do what others do here. We are no longer in the mountains of the West, Mama, where everyone eats potatoes. We are in the city now. So would you—Mama, would you please leave out the potatoes?"

"No potatoes," Mama said thoughtfully. She looked at Maria's anxious face. She shrugged. "Well, there are plenty of good things in the Mexicali Soup without potatoes. I will add more of everything else. It will still make good soup."

Maria kissed Mama's cheek. "Of course it will, Mama. You make the best soup in the world."

Mama went on with Juanita to the markets, to the street of little markets, thinking aloud as she went. "Tomatoes, onions, celery. Red peppers, chili peppers, good and hot. And garlic. But no potatoes."

Mama went to Mr. Santini's little market for the best tomatoes and celery. She went to Mr. Vierra's little market for the best onions and garlic. "And the peppers," she said to Juanita. "We will buy the peppers from Antonio. Our own Antonio, at the market of Mr. Fernandez. Here is the place. Ah! What beautiful peppers!"

Antonio came hurrying out of the store to the little stand on the sidewalk.

"Let me help you, Mama! I hope you want something very good for our supper tonight. I get very hungry working here," Antonio said.

"Ah, *si!*" Mama said. "Yes, Antonio. For tonight—something special!" She reached for the hot red peppers strung above her head. "Mexicali Soup."

"Hey! That's great," Antonio exclaimed. Then he looked thoughtful. Then he frowned. "But—Mama—"

"Yes?" Mama said, putting some peppers in the scale.

"Well—Mama, you use a lot of hot peppers in your soup."

"Of course," Mama said, smiling.

"A lot," Antonio repeated. "Too many, Mama. People here don't do that. They don't cook that way. They don't eat the way we did in the mountains of the West. I know, Mama. I have worked here for weeks now, after school and Saturdays. And in all that time, Mama, I have not sold as many hot peppers to other ladies as you use in a week.

"*Mamacita*," Antonio said. "Please don't put hot peppers in the soup."

"No peppers," Mama said thoughtfully. She looked at Antonio's anxious face. "Well—" Mama shrugged. "There are plenty of good things in the soup without peppers. I will add more of something else. It will still make good soup."

Antonio took the peppers out of the scale and put them back on the stand. "Of course it will, Mama." He kissed her cheek. "Everyone knows you make the best soup in the world."

Mama went on with Juanita toward home. "Tomatoes, onions, garlic, celery," she said to herself. "Yes. I can still make a good soup with those."

She hummed softly to herself as she crossed a street blocked off from traffic, a street that was only for play.

"Hey, Mama! *Mamacita!*"

Juan and Manuel left the game of stickball in the play street. They raced each other to the spot where Mama stood.

"Oh, boy! Food!" said Juan when he saw the bags in the stroller. He opened one of the bags. "Tomatoes and celery—I know what that means."

"Me, too," said Manuel. He peeked into the other bag. "Onions and garlic. Mexicali Soup! Right, Mama?" Manuel rubbed his stomach and grinned. Then he looked thoughtful. Then he frowned. "But, Mama—listen, Mama."

"I am listening," Mama said.

"Well, I think we use an awful lot of onions," Manuel said. "They don't use so many onions in the lunchroom at school, or at the Boys' Club picnics. You know, Mama, they have different ways of doing things here, different from the ways of our town on the side of the mountain. I think we should try new ways. I think we shouldn't use so many onions. *Mamacita*, please make the Mexicali Soup without onions."

"Manuel is right!" Juan said. "My teacher said only today that there is nothing that cannot be changed, and there is nothing so good that it cannot be made better, if we will only try. I think there may be better ways of making soup than our old way. Make the soup tonight without tomatoes, Mama!"

"No tomatoes?" Mama said. "And no onions? In Mexicali Soup?" Mama looked at the anxious faces of Juan and Manuel. Then she shrugged. She closed the two bags of groceries carefully. She pushed the stroller away from the play street. She shrugged again.

Voices came after her. Juan's voice said, "We will be hungry for your soup tonight, Mama!"

Manuel's voice called, "*Mamacita!* You make the best soup in the world!"

In the big kitchen at home, Mama put the groceries on the table by the stove. She hummed a little soft tune that only Mama could hear. She stood looking at the groceries. No potatoes. No peppers. Tomatoes—Mama pushed the tomatoes aside. Onions—she pushed the onions aside.

Mama sat down and looked at what was left.

The front door clicked open and shut. Rosie came into the kitchen. Rosita, the young lady of the family.

"Hi, Mama. Oh, Mama—I hope I'm in time! I heard you were making—" Rosie stopped to catch her breath. She frowned at the groceries on the table. "All the way home I heard it. The boys and Maria—they all told me—and Mama! I want to ask you—please! No garlic."

Mama stopped humming.

Rosie turned up her nose and spread out her hands. "No garlic. Please. Listen, Mama. Last night, when my friend took me to dinner, I had such a fine soup! Delicious! The place was so elegant, Mama—so refined. So expensive. And no garlic at all in the soup!"

Rosie bent over and kissed Mama's cheek. "Just leave out the garlic, *Mamacita*. You make the best soup in the world."

A deep voice and many other voices called all at once, and the front door shut with a bang. "Mama! We are home, Mama!"

Then all of them, Juan and Manuel and Antonio, with Maria pulling Papa by the hand—all of them came to stand in the kitchen doorway. Papa reached for the baby, the little Juanita, and swung her onto his shoulders.

"I have heard of something special," Papa said. "I have heard we are having Mexicali Soup tonight."

Mama said nothing. But Mama's eyes flashed fire. She waited.

"Your soup, Mama—" Papa said. "It is simply the best soup in the world!"

"Ah, *si!* But you want me to leave out something?" Mama's voice rose high. "The celery, perhaps? You want me to make my Mexicali Soup without the celery?"

Papa raised his eyebrows. "Celery?" Papa opened his hands wide and shrugged. "What is celery? It is a little nothing! Put it in or leave it out, *Mamacita*—it does not matter. The soup will be just as—"

"Enough!" Mama said. "Out of my kitchen—all of you!"

Mama waved her arms wide in the air. The fire in Mama's eyes flashed again. "I am busy! I am busy getting your supper. I will call you. Go."

"But, Mama," said Rosie, "we always help you with—"

"No!" Mama said. "Out!"

Rosie and Juan and Manuel, Antonio and Maria, and Papa with the baby, tiptoed away to the living room.

There was only silence coming from the kitchen. Then, the sound of a quiet humming. Soon the humming mixed with the clatter of plates and spoons, the good sounds of the table being set for supper.

The humming turned into singing. Mama was singing a happy song from the old home in the mountains. Juan and Manuel, Antonio and Maria, Rosie and Papa, looked at one another and smiled and nodded. Mama was singing.

Then from the kitchen Mama's voice called to them.

"The soup is finished. Your supper is ready. Come and eat now."

"Ah! That is what I like to hear," said Papa, jumping up with Juanita. "The soup is ready before I have even begun to smell it cooking."

"Mmm-mmm!" said Juan and Manuel, racing for the big kitchen table.

"Mmm-mmm!" said Maria and Antonio and Rosie, when they saw the steaming bowls on the table. "Mama makes the best soup in the world."

But what was the matter?

"This doesn't look like Mexicali Soup," said Maria, staring at the bowl before her.

"It doesn't smell like Mexicali Soup," said Antonio, sniffing the steam that rose from his bowl.

"It doesn't taste like Mexicali Soup," said Juan and Manuel, sipping a sip from their spoons.

"This is not Mexicali Soup," said Rosie, setting her spoon down hard with a clang. "This is nothing but hot water!"

Everyone looked at Mama.

Mama smiled and hummed the old tune from the mountains.

"You have forgotten to bring the soup, *Mamacita?*" suggested Papa.

"No," Mama said, still smiling. "The soup is in your bowls. And it is just what you wanted. I made the soup the way my family asked me to make it. I left out the potatoes that Maria does not want. I left out the peppers Antonio does not want. I left out the tomatoes that Juan does not want. I left out the onions that Manuel does not want. For Rosita, I left out the garlic. And for Papa, I left out the celery, the little nothing that does not matter.

"The *new* Mexicali Soup! It is so simple! So quick! So easy to make," Mama said. "You just leave everything out of it."

Use with Grade 1, Chapter 5, Lesson 3

Math Songs
Side 2, Selection 3

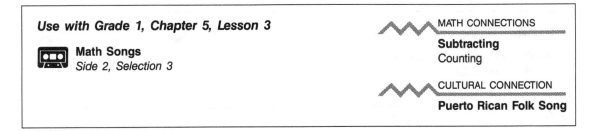

MATH CONNECTIONS

Subtracting
Counting

CULTURAL CONNECTION

Puerto Rican Folk Song

Ten Puppies *(Diez Perritos)*

This Puerto Rican folk song focuses on the concept of one less. You may want to reacquaint children with the numbers 1 to 10 in the Spanish language by playing the "Counting Song."

Puerto Rican Folk Song

1. Oh, I used to have ten pup - pies,
Yo te - ní - a diez pe - rri - tos,
yō te nē' ä dyes pe rē' tōs

Oh, I used to have ten pup - pies;
Yo te - ní - a diez pe - rri - tos;
yō te nē' ä dyes pe rē' tōs

One fell in the snow so fine,
U - no se ca yó en la nie - ve
ōo' nō sā kä yō'en lä nye' ve

Leav-ing me with on - ly nine.
ya - no mas me que dan nue - ve.
yä nō mäs mä kä' dän nōōe' ve

2. Oh, I used to have nine puppies,
   Oh, I used to have nine puppies;
   One went running through the gate,
   Leaving me with only eight.

3. . . .eight. . .One went flying up to heaven, . . .seven.

4. . . .seven. . .One went running after sticks, . . .six.

5. . . .six. . .One went out to take a drive, . . .five.

6. . . .five. . .One was left outside the door, . . .four.

7. . . .four. . .One was barking at a tree, . . .three.

8. . . .three. . .One was chewing on a shoe, . . .two.

9. . . .two. . .One went running just for fun, . . .one.

10. . . .one. . .One went chasing a brown cow,
    So I have no puppy now.

Use with Grade 1, Chapter 6, Lesson 1

 Read-Aloud Selections
Grade 1, Tape 1
Side 2, Selection 3

MATH CONNECTIONS

Adding
Counting

Bleezer's Ice Cream

FROM *THE NEW KID ON THE BLOCK*
BY JACK PRELUTSKY

Bleezer's Ice Cream Store has 28 different flavors. If each of the children in your class created a flavor, how many would there be? Grouping the flavors in a variety of ways also can give children practice in adding 2-digit numbers.

I am Ebenezer Bleezer,
I run BLEEZER'S ICE CREAM STORE.
there are flavors in my freezer
you have never seen before,
twenty-eight divine creations
too delicious to resist,
why not do yourself a favor,
try the flavors on my list:

COCOA MOCHA MACARONI
TAPIOCA SMOKED BALONEY
CHECKERBERRY CHEDDAR CHEW
CHICKEN CHERRY HONEYDEW
TUTTI-FRUTTI STEWED TOMATO
TUNA TACO BAKED POTATO
LOBSTER LITCHI LIMA BEAN
MOZZARELLA MANGOSTEEN
ALMOND HAM MERINGUE SALAMI
YAM ANCHOVY PRUNE PASTRAMI
SASSAFRAS SOUVLAKI HASH
SUKIYAKI SUCCOTASH
BUTTER BRICKLE PEPPER PICKLE
POMEGRANATE PUMPERNICKEL
PEACH PIMENTO PIZZA PLUM
PEANUT PUMPKIN BUBBLEGUM
BROCCOLI BANANA BLUSTER
CHOCOLATE CHOP SUEY CLUSTER
AVOCADO BRUSSELS SPROUT
PERIWINKLE SAUERKRAUT
COTTON CANDY CARROT CUSTARD
CAULIFLOWER COLA MUSTARD
ONION DUMPLING DOUBLE DIP
TURNIP TRUFFLE TRIPLE FLIP
GARLIC GUMBO GRAVY GUAVA
LENTIL LEMON LIVER LAVA
ORANGE OLIVE BAGEL BEET
WATERMELON WAFFLE WHEAT

I am Ebenezer Bleezer,
I run BLEEZER'S ICE CREAM STORE.
taste a flavor from my freezer,
you will surely ask for more.

Hugs and Kisses

BY CHARLOTTE POMERANTZ

Charlotte Pomerantz introduces the number 30 in both English and Spanish. The discussion of time in this poem also presents excellent opportunities for working with a calendar.

Mami, how long will you be away?

  I'll be gone for a month, María.

Then give me a kiss for every day,
For every day that you are away.

  That's thirty small kisses, María.
  Treinta besitos, one for each day.
  One for each day that I am away.
  Treinta besitos, María.

Now give me a hug for every day,
For every day that you are away.

  That's thirty big hugs, María.
  Treinta abrazos, one for each day.
  One for each day that I am away.
  Treinta abrazos, María.

Now give me a doll for every day,
For every day that you are away.

  That's thirty dollies, María.
  Treinta muñecas, one for each day.
  One for each day that I am away.
  No, indeed, María.

88

The Ants at the Olympics

BY RICHARD DIGANCE

There are 62 teams at the Jungle Olympics, and the ants always come in last! The mention of the month of August and New Year's Day in the eighth stanza can lead to discussions of time.

At last year's Jungle Olympics,
the Ants were completely outclassed.
In fact, from an entry of sixty-two teams,
the Ants came their usual last.

They didn't win one single medal.
Not that that's a surprise.
The reason was not lack of trying,
but more their unfortunate size.

While the cheetahs won most of the sprinting
and the hippos won putting the shot,
the Ants tried sprinting but couldn't,
and tried to put but could not.

It was sad for the ants 'cause they're sloggers.
They turn out for every event.
With their shorts and their bright orange tee-shirts,
their athletes are proud they are sent.

They came in last at the high jump and hurdles,
which they say they'd have won, but they fell.
They came in last in the four hundred meters
and last in the swimming as well.

They came in last in the long-distance running,
though they say they might have come first.
And they might if the other sixty-one teams
hadn't put in a finishing burst.

But each year they turn up regardless.
They're popular in the parade.
The other teams whistle and cheer them,
aware of the journey they've made.

For the Jungle Olympics in August,
they have to set off New Year's Day.
They didn't arrive the year before last.
They set off but went the wrong way.

So long as they try there's a reason.
After all, it's only a sport.
They'll be back next year to bring up the rear,
and that's an encouraging thought.

Use with Grade 1, Chapter 7, Lesson 1

 Read-Aloud Selections
Grade 1, Tape 1
Side 2, Selection 4

MATH CONNECTIONS

Money
Adding
Multiplying

Mud Fore Sale

BY BRENDA NELSON

*Some children sell lemonade in the summer, but not Max! He sells mud for two cents!
To help your children visualize the misspelled sign mentioned in this story, draw the following sign on the chalkboard at the appropriate moment.*

> MUD
> FORE SALE
> 2¢

*Draw an X through the E in the word FORE as you read the words ". . .and made a
big X on his sign."*

It was summer, and all of Max's friends were selling something.

Ben was selling worms.

Zack was selling flowers.

Pam was selling kittens.

Max wanted to sell something, too, but he didn't know what to sell. Max
asked Pam if he could help sell kittens.

"Only if you buy one first," she said.

"No, thanks," Max said.

He asked Ben if he could help sell worms.

Ben said, "You can help me dig them."

"OK," Max said.

He took Ben's shovel and started to dig.

Suddenly, he stopped digging. He looked at the dirt. He had a wonderful idea.

Max told Ben, "I can't dig worms now; I have something else to do. See you
later." And he ran home.

Max took two big pails and filled them with dirt. Then he put in water and mixed it up. Next Max took a pen and some paper, and he printed:

MUD FORE SALE 2¢

He took his pails and his sign and put them by the sidewalk. Then he sat down to wait. Max hadn't sat very long when a man walked by.

"Do you want some mud?" Max asked.

"No, thank you," said the man, and kept on walking.

A boy rode up on his bike. He stopped. He looked at the mud. He took out two cents and gave them to Max.

Max said, "Help yourself."

The boy took the mud and printed his name on the sidewalk. As he got on his bike he said to Max, "You don't spell very good." And he rode away.

"Who cares?" Max said. Then he looked at the sign. He shut one eye, and then the other eye. "I know," Max said. He took some mud and made a big X on his sign.

Max sat and sat. He got tired of waiting for someone to come. He took some mud and painted his legs. He painted his arms. He painted his face. He was putting stripes on his shirt when Ben and Zack came over.

"That looks like fun," Zack said. "Can we do it, too?"

"Give me two cents," Max said.

"OK," they said.

Zack painted Ben. Ben painted Zack.

Mrs. Topp came out in her yard. "Does your mother know what you are doing?" she asked Max.

"I don't know," Max said.

"I don't think she'll be happy," she said, and went back in her house.

Max looked at his six cents. He looked at Ben and Zack. He looked at his house.

"I'm done selling mud," he said. "Let's clean up with the hose."

Max sprayed Zack. Zack sprayed Ben. Ben was spraying Max when Max's mother looked out the door. She said, "What are you doing?"

Max said, "Getting wet."

"I can see that," she said, "but you're done now."

Ben and Zack went home.

Max asked his mother, "Would you get mad if I sold mud?"

"Mud!" his mother said. "Don't you dare!"

"OK," Max said.

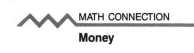
A Poem for a Pickle

BY EVE MERRIAM

With Eve Merriam's poem as a guide, the children can exchange pennies for nickels and nickels for dimes.

Five pennies for a nickel,
a poem for a pickle.

Two nickels for a dime,
a rhyme to pass the time.

Four quarters for a one,
a couplet just for fun

and I'll keep the change.

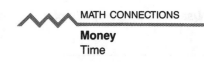
Fifteen Cents

BY ANONYMOUS

This poem can lead children to investigate which combinations of coins can make up fifteen cents.

I asked my mother for fifteen cents
To see the elephant jump the fence,
He jumped so high that he touched the sky
And never came back 'till the Fourth of July.

Use with Grade 1, Chapter 7, Lesson 2

 Math Songs
Side 2, Selection 4

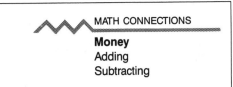 MATH CONNECTIONS
Money
Adding
Subtracting

Pop Goes the Weasel

You can use this American singing game to talk about pennies.

American Singing Game

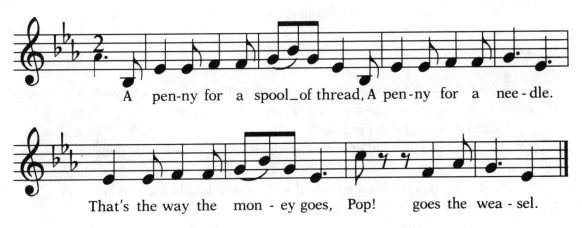

A pen-ny for a spool_of thread, A pen-ny for a nee - dle.

That's the way the mon - ey goes, Pop! goes the wea - sel.

Use with Grade 1, Chapter 8, Lesson 1

 Read-Aloud Selections
Grade 1, Tape 2
Side 1, Selection 1

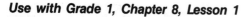 MATH CONNECTIONS

Measuring
Time
Geometry

Two Loaves

FROM *I DID IT,* BY HARLOW ROCKWELL

As Harlow Rockwell's story demonstrates so well, baking bread involves measurement, time, and even geometry!

I poured one and a half cups of warm water into the big mixing bowl. I added a teaspoon of salt and a package of dry yeast. I stirred.

I added a cup of flour. I stirred.

I added three more cups of flour and stirred some more. I made dough.

I sprinkled some flour on the kitchen table. I put the dough on the table.

I folded the dough toward me like this. And then I pushed it away, like this. I kneaded the dough. I kneaded for ten minutes.

Then I put the dough in the bowl. I covered the bowl with a warm, damp dishtowel. And then I went outside to play.

Two hours later I looked at the dough. There was more of it. The dough was twice as big as it was before!

I punched the dough down with my fist. It was full of bubbles and it squished like an old balloon.

I smeared some cooking oil on a cookie sheet. I made two round balls of dough. I put them on the cookie sheet.

I read a book, and drew a picture, and played with my dog.

Forty-five minutes later I looked. The balls of dough were bigger.

I turned on the oven to three hundred and fifty degrees. In fifteen minutes I put the cookie sheets with the balls of dough into the oven.

In forty minutes I smelled something good. The balls of dough were big and brown. They were not soft any more. They were loaves of bread now.

I took the bread out of the oven. Everybody ate some while it was still warm.

Now I am a baker. I made bread.

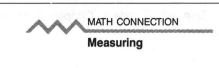

MATH CONNECTION
Measuring

Spring Is Coming

The first sign of spring in this song is the pussy willows. What signals the coming of spring to your children?

*Words and music by
Milton Kaye*

Spring   is   com - ing, Spring   is   com - ing,

How   do   you   think   I   know?_____

I   saw   some   pus - sy   wil - lows,

I   know   it   must   be   so.

97

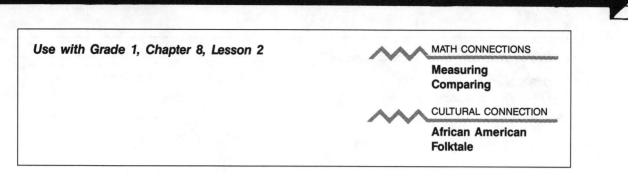

MATH CONNECTIONS
Measuring
Comparing

CULTURAL CONNECTION
African American
Folktale

The Knee-High Man

AN AFRICAN AMERICAN FOLKTALE RETOLD BY JULIUS LESTER

The knee-high man in this African American folktale constantly compares himself to bigger animals. A wise owl helps him to come to terms with his size. Children may enjoy creating their own knee-high people to use as a nonstandard measurement.

Once upon a time there was a knee-high man. He was no taller than a person's knees. Because he was so short, he was very unhappy. He wanted to be big like everybody else.

One day he decided to ask the biggest animal he could find how he could get big. So he went to see Mr. Horse. "Mr. Horse, how can I get big like you?"

Mr. Horse said, "Well, eat a whole lot of corn. Then run around a lot. After a while you'll be as big as me."

The knee-high man did just that. He ate so much corn that his stomach hurt. Then he ran and ran and ran until his legs hurt. But he didn't get any bigger. So he decided that Mr. Horse had told him something wrong. He decided to go ask Mr. Bull.

"Mr. Bull? How can I get big like you?"

Mr. Bull said, "Eat a whole lot of grass. Then bellow and bellow as loud as you can. The first thing you know, you'll be as big as me."

So the knee-high man ate a whole field of grass. That made his stomach hurt. He bellowed and bellowed and bellowed all day and all night. That made his throat hurt. But he didn't get any bigger. So he decided that Mr. Bull was all wrong too.

Now he didn't know anyone else to ask. One night he heard Mr. Hoot Owl hooting, and he remembered that Mr. Owl knew everything. "Mr. Owl? How can I get big like Mr. Horse and Mr. Bull?"

"What do you want to be big for?" Mr. Hoot Owl asked.

"I want to be big so that when I get into a fight, I can whip everybody," the knee-high man said.

Mr. Hoot Owl hooted. "Anybody ever try to pick a fight with you?"

The knee-high man thought a minute. "Well, now that you mention it, nobody ever did try to start a fight with me."

Mr. Owl said, "Well, you don't have any reason to fight. Therefore, you don't have any reason to be bigger than you are."

"But, Mr. Owl," the knee-high man said, "I want to be big so I can see far into the distance."

Mr. Hoot Owl hooted. "If you climb a tall tree, you can see into the distance from the top."

The knee-high man was quiet for a minute. "Well, I hadn't thought of that."

Mr. Hoot Owl hooted again. "And that's what's wrong, Mr. Knee-High Man. You hadn't done any thinking at all. I'm smaller than you, and you don't see me worrying about being big. Mr. Knee-High Man, you wanted something that you didn't need."

Use with Grade 1, Chapter 9, Lesson 1

 Read-Aloud Selections
Grade 1, Tape 2
Side 1, Selection 2

MATH CONNECTIONS
Adding
Subtracting
Counting
Money
Time

Morris Goes to School

BY B. WISEMAN

This story contains several sight jokes which you will need to explain. The jokes are contained in parentheses within the story. Morris's adventures with money and counting can increase children's awareness of one-to-one correspondence and adding.

Morris the Moose wanted candy. He went to the wrong store.

(The illustration shows Morris walking into a fish store. The letters F I S H are clearly visible in the window.)

The man in the store said, "We don't sell candy. Can't you read?" Then he showed Morris the candy store.

The man in the candy store said, "What would you like?"

Morris looked at the candy. He liked the gumdrops. He said, "Give me some of those."

The man said, "They are one for a penny. How much money do you have?"

Morris looked. He had six pennies. "I have four pennies," he said.

The man laughed. "You have six! Can't you count? Don't you go to school?"

Morris asked, "What is school?"

The man said, "I will show you. But first, here are six gumdrops. They are one for a penny, and you have six pennies."

Then the man took Morris to school. The children said, "Oh, look! A real moose!"

The teacher said, "Hello. My name is Miss Fine."

The man said, "He never went to school."

Morris could not say anything. His mouth was full of gumdrops. Morris swallowed his gumdrops. Then he said, "My name is Morris the Moose. I want to learn to count. I want to learn to read, too. I like candy!"

Miss Fine said, "Hello, Morris. Welcome to our class. Please sit at a desk."

Morris tried, but he didn't fit. He had to sit on top of the desk.

"We will now study the alphabet," said Miss Fine. "This is an *A*. This is a *B* . . ."

Morris hid under the desk. He yelled, "Where is the bee? I'm afraid of bees! They sting!"

Miss Fine said, "I meant the letter *B*. This one here. It doesn't sting."

Then Miss Fine said, "And next there is *C*. . . ."

"Oh, I like the sea!" Morris said. "I love to swim!"

"No, no!" said Miss Fine. "I meant the letter *C*. This one here. And next," Miss Fine said, "there is *D*, and *E*, and *F, G, H, I* . ."

Morris yelled, "I have an eye! I have two of them!"

Miss Fine said, "I meant the letter *I*. Morris, please don't interrupt again."

Morris didn't. Morris couldn't. Morris wasn't there. He had to leave the room.

One door said BOYS. One door said GIRLS. Morris couldn't read yet. He opened the wrong door.

A girl cried, "Stop! You can't come in here! This is for girls. The other one is for boys."

Morris told Miss Fine, "There is no door for a moose!"

Miss Fine put up a sign.

(The sign she posts reads: Boys and Moose!*)*

When Morris came back, Miss Fine said, "Now we will spell. *Cat* is spelled *C-A-T. Dog* is spelled *D-O-G.*"

Morris looked sad.

"What is the matter, Morris?" asked Miss Fine.

Morris said, "You didn't spell *moose.*"

"Can anyone spell *moose?*" asked Miss Fine.

A boy said, "*M-O-S-E!*"

A girl said, "No, no! It is *M-O-O-C-E!*"

"You are both wrong," said Miss Fine. "It is spelled *M-O-O-S-E.*"

Morris said, "Oh, I am hard to spell!"

Miss Fine said, "I think it is time for lunch."

The children opened their lunch boxes. Some of them had cheese sandwiches. Some had cream cheese and jelly sandwiches. Some had hamburgers. Each of them had a piece of fruit.

But Morris had nothing! He ate lunch anyway.

(The illustration shows Morris leaning out the window, nibbling the grass in the schoolyard.)

After lunch the children played. Some played ball and some jumped rope. Morris did both at the same time.

Miss Fine said, "Children, now it is time to rest."

The children rested on their desks. Morris tried, but he was too big. Miss Fine let him use her desk.

When rest time was over, Miss Fine said, "Wake up! Wake up! It is time to finger-paint."

Morris said, "I will hoof-paint!" You can tell which painting he did.

(The illustration depicts several paintings of hand prints. One painting has a hoof print.)

Miss Fine said, "Now we will study arithmetic. Who would like to count?"

A boy counted, "1, 2, 3, 4, 5, 6, 7, 8, 10 . ."

"No, no!" said Miss Fine. "Who knows what comes after eight?"

Morris said, "I know! Bedtime!"

"Nine is the answer," said Miss Fine. "Nine comes after eight. Who knows what comes after nine?"

A girl counted on her fingers. "1, 2, 3, 4, 5, 6, 7, 8, 9, 10. Ten!" she said. "Ten comes after nine."

Miss Fine said, "That's right."

Morris looked sad.

"What is the matter, Morris?" asked Miss Fine.

Morris held up his hoofs. "I can only count to four," he said.

Miss Fine said, "You can count higher than that. I will show you." She counted on Morris's hoofs. "1, 2, 3, 4 . ." Then she counted on Morris's antlers. ". . . 5, 6, 7, 8, 9, 10, 11, 12."

Morris said, "I like to count. I will never wear a hat."

Miss Fine said, "Now I think it is time to sing a song."

"What is a song?" Morris asked.

Miss Fine said, "I will show you." She sang: "I've been working on the railroad . . ."

"What is a railroad?" Morris asked.

"A railroad has tracks," said Miss Fine. "They look like this."

(Miss Fine draws two parallel lines horizontally on the board. The horizontal lines are joined by several vertical lines. These lines resemble a ladder on its side.)

"Oh, I know what tracks are," Morris said. "Firemen climb them!"

"No, no," said Miss Fine. "Firemen climb ladders. Ladders go up, like this."

Morris said, "Let's sing another song. I'm learning a lot!"

Miss Fine said, "No. We just have time for a game. Let's play make-believe!"

A girl said, "I am a TREE!"

A boy said, "I am a MONKEY!"

Another boy said, "I am a MOOSE!"

(The illustration shows a boy holding his hands upright behind his head to indicate that he has antlers.)

Morris and the children laughed. Morris went to the coat closet. He said, "I am a COAT CLOSET!"

(The illustration shows Morris with coats, scarves, and hats draped over his antlers and arms.)

The children laughed again. Miss Fine laughed, too. Then the school bell rang.

Morris asked, "Is that the ice-cream man?"

Miss Fine said, "No. It is time to go home."

Morris gave the children their coats. The children and Morris said, "Good-bye, Miss Fine."

Miss Fine said, "I will see you all tomorrow."

Morris ran to the forest. He took money from his hiding place. He wanted candy. This time he went to the right store. He said, "Hello. I want some gumdrops, please."

The man said, "Hello. They are one for a penny. How much money do you have?"

Morris looked. He had five pennies. "I have five pennies," he said. "Give me five gumdrops, please."

The man gave Morris the gumdrops. He said, "You have learned arithmetic! What else have you learned in school?"

Morris said, "I learned how to hoof-paint. I learned how to spell *moose*. I learned how to be a clothes closet. And I learned all the numbers in the alphabet!"

The man said, "You mean all the LETTERS, don't you?"

Morris wanted to say Yes. Morris tried to say Yes. But Morris couldn't. His mouth was full of gumdrops.

Cottage

BY ELEANOR FARJEON

Which groups of animals and/or objects add up to 12?

When I live in a Cottage
I shall keep in my Cottage

Two different Dogs,
Three creamy Cows,
Four giddy Goats,
Five Pewter Pots,
Six silver Spoons,
Seven busy Beehives,
Eight ancient Appletrees,
Nine red Rosebushes,
Ten teeming Teapots,
Eleven chirping Chickens,
Twelve cosy Cats with their kittenish
    Kittens and
One blessed Baby in a Basket.

That's what I'll have when I live in my
Cottage.

Use with Grade 1, Chapter 10, Lesson 1

 Read-Aloud Selections
Grade 1, Tape 2
Side 1, Selection 3

MATH CONNECTION
Time

A List

FROM *FROG AND TOAD TOGETHER* BY ARNOLD LOBEL

Toad makes a list of all the things he has to do. Everything is fine until the list blows away, and he can't remember what to do!

One morning Toad sat in bed. "I have many things to do," he said. "I will write them all down on a list so that I can remember them."

Toad wrote on a piece of paper:

A List of things to do today

Then he wrote:

Wake up

"I have done that," said Toad, and he crossed out:

W̶a̶k̶e̶ ̶u̶p̶

Then Toad wrote other things on the paper.

"There," said Toad. "Now my day is all written down."

He got out of bed and had something to eat. Then Toad crossed out:

E̶a̶t̶ ̶B̶r̶e̶a̶k̶f̶a̶s̶t̶

a List of things to do today

Wake up
Eat Breakfast
Get Dressed
Go to Frog's House
Take walk with Frog
Eat lunch
Take nap
Play games with Frog
Eat Supper
Go to Sleep

Toad took his clothes out of the closet and put them on. Then he crossed out:

~~Get Dressed~~

Toad put the list in his pocket. He opened the door and walked out into the morning. Soon Toad was at Frog's front door. He took the list from his pocket and crossed out:

~~Go to Frog's House~~

Toad knocked at the door.
"Hello," said Frog.
"Look at my list of things to do," said Toad.
"Oh," said Frog, "that is very nice."
Toad said, "My list tells me that we will go for a walk."
"All right," said Frog. "I am ready."
Frog and Toad went on a long walk. Then Toad took the list from his pocket again. He crossed out:

~~Take walk with Frog~~

Just then there was a strong wind. It blew the list out of Toad's hand. The list blew high up into the air. "Help!" cried Toad. "My list is blowing away. What will I do without my list?"
"Hurry!" said Frog. "We will run and catch it."
"No!" shouted Toad. "I cannot do that."
"Why not?" asked Frog.
"Because," wailed Toad, "running after my list is not one of the things that I wrote on my list of things to do!"
Frog ran after the list. He ran over hills and swamps, but the list blew on and on. At last Frog came back to Toad. "I am sorry," gasped Frog, "but I could not catch your list."
"Blah," said Toad. "I cannot remember any of the things that were on my list of things to do. I will just have to sit here and do nothing," said Toad.

Toad sat and did nothing. Frog sat with him. After a long time Frog said, "Toad, it is getting dark. We should be going to sleep now."

"Go to sleep!" shouted Toad. "That was the last thing on my list!"

Toad wrote on the ground with a stick:

Go to sleep

Then he crossed out:

G̶o̶ t̶o̶ s̶l̶e̶e̶p̶

"There," said Toad. "Now my day is all crossed out!"

"I am glad," said Frog.

Then Frog and Toad went right to sleep.

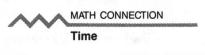
The Oak Tree

BY LAURA JANE COATS

Laura Jane Coats chronicles the sequence of events that occurs near an oak tree in 24 hours.

At six o'clock the sun comes up,
Baby birds in a nest wait for their breakfast.

At eight o'clock a squirrel gathers acorns.
Then he hurries off to hide them.

At ten o'clock a cow wanders by
and pauses to scratch her back.

At twelve o'clock children play croquet
and picnic in the shade.

At two o'clock a cloud brings rain. But before long
a rainbow appears, and the sun comes out again.

At four o'clock a boy climbs up among
the branches and looks out over the hillside.

At six o'clock the sun goes down,
and as it does the moon begins to rise.

At eight o'clock a traveler takes off his pack
and rolls out his bed for the night.

At twelve o'clock an owl watches
a mouse on the moonlit hill.

At two o'clock a possum family
creeps over the hill and slips away.

At four o'clock the traveler awakes.
Soon he is packed and on his way.

And at six o'clock, as the moon goes down,
the sun comes up to begin another day.

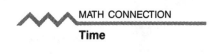
The Face of the Clock

BY PHYLLIS McGINLEY

Using an analog clock to mirror the words of the poem will allow children to see the special relationship between the minute hand and the hour hand.

1. The Big Hand is busy
   But the Small Hand has power.
   The Large one counts the minutes.
   But the Little one names the hour.
   Which only goes to show us all
   That Big's no better off than Small.

2. When both Hands stand at the top together,
   It's sure to be TWELVE O'CLOCK. But whether
   That's twelve at noon or twelve at night
   Depends on if it's dark or light.

3. NINE and THREE
   Are easy to see.
   The Big Hand's up
   As high as can be,
   Straight as a soldier,
   Guarding a town.

   At THREE
   The Little Hand's
   Halfway down,
   Like the soldier's gun
   Before he drops it.

110

But NINE O'CLOCK
Is exactly opp'site.
Perhaps you're at school
Perhaps at play
Or else in bed
At the end of day,
But it's NINE O'CLOCK
Upon the crack
When the Brave Little Hand
Climbs halfway back.

4. When down to the bottom the Little Hand goes,
   Up top the Big Hand's steady,
Come in, spick-spock!
For it's SIX O'CLOCK
   And supper is probably ready.

5. Some folks believe that we should have *more* o'clock,
Since midnight's really TWENTY-FOUR O'CLOCK.
But dials like that? You never see 'em.
There's only TWELVE A.M. or P.M.

Perhaps here's all it may amount to:
TWELVE is the highest clocks can count to.

Use with Grade 1, Chapter 10, Lesson 6

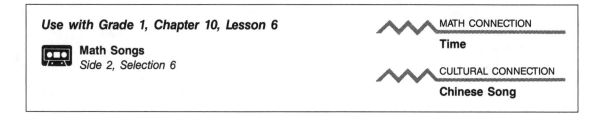

Math Songs
Side 2, Selection 6

MATH CONNECTION
Time

CULTURAL CONNECTION
Chinese Song

Ai Hai Yo

This song celebrating the Chinese New Year originated in the Shansi province of northern China. Children may enjoy learning about where Chinese New Year falls on the calendar.

Shansi Melody

A

End (Fine)

Ai hai yo Ai hai yo Ai hai yo hai yo.

B

Land of drag-ons and the sun, the New Year has be-gun.

Go back to the beginning and sing to the End (Da Capo al Fine)

In our homes and fields we will have a good year.

Use with Grade 1, Chapter 11, Lesson 1

 Read-Aloud Selections
Grade 1, Tape 2
Side 2, Selection 1

MATH CONNECTIONS

Geometry
Comparing
Measuring

The Most Wonderful Egg in the World

BY HELME HEINE

Which egg is the most wonderful egg in the world? Is it the most beautiful egg, the biggest egg, or the egg shaped like a square?

ONCE UPON A TIME, a long time ago, three hens were quarreling about which of them was the most beautiful.

Dotty had the most beautiful feathers. Stalky had the most beautiful legs. And Plumy had the most beautiful crest.

Since they could not settle their quarrel among themselves, they decided to ask the king for his advice.

"What you can do is more important than what you look like," said the king. "Whichever one of you lays the most wonderful egg I will make a princess."

He went out into the palace park followed by all the hens in his kingdom.

Dotty preened her beautiful feathers before settling herself in the wet grass. It was not long before she cackled, stood up, and stepped aside.

Everybody was speechless. There lay an egg, snow-white, spotless, and perfectly shaped—the eggshell shimmering like polished marble. "This is the most perfect egg I have ever seen," cried the king," and all the hens nodded.

Then it was Stalky's turn. Everybody felt a little sorry for her. They knew she could not lay a more perfect egg. It was impossible.

After ten minutes Stalky cackled, got up, and stretched her legs proudly in the morning sun.

The king clapped his hands for joy. There lay an egg of such size and weight that even an ostrich would have been jealous.

"This is the biggest egg I have ever seen," cried the king, and all the hens nodded.

While they were still nodding, Plumy settled herself carefully on the ground. Everybody felt extremely sorry for her. They knew she could not lay a more perfect or bigger egg. It was unthinkable. Modestly, with castdown eyes, she sat there.

Then, with only a small cackle, she got up to reveal an egg that would be talked about for the next hundred years.

Before them lay a square egg. Each side was straight, as if drawn with a ruler, and each surface shone in a different color.

"This is indeed the most fantastic egg I have ever seen," cried the king, and all the hens nodded.

It was impossible to say which egg was the most wonderful. So the king decided that all three hens—Dotty, Stalky, and Plumy—should be made princesses.

And from that day to this they have been the best of friends, and have happily gone on laying extraordinary eggs.

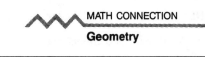
Animals' Houses

BY JAMES REEVES

Displaying pictures of the animals' houses described in this poem will enhance children's appreciation of geometric shapes.

Of animals' houses
    Two sorts are found—
Those which are square ones
    And those which are round.

Square is a hen-house,
    A kennel, a sty:
Cows have square houses
    And so have I.

A snail's shell is curly,
    A bird's nest round;
Rabbits have twisty burrows
    Underground.

But the fish in the bowl
    And the fish at sea—
Their houses are round
    As a house can be.

115

Use with Grade 1, Chapter 12, Lesson 1

 Read-Aloud Selections
Grade 1, Tape 2
Side 2, Selection 2

 MATH CONNECTIONS

Adding
Subtracting
Multiplying
Dividing
Number Sense

Too Many Hopkins

BY TOMIE dePAOLA

Grouping the Hopkins in various ways can prepare the children for multiplication and division, and it can also strengthen their addition and subtraction skills.

"Well," said Daddy Hopkins, looking out at the fine spring morning. "It's time to plant our gardens."

"This year, Daddy and I want all of you children to help," said Mommy Hopkins.

"Oh, goody!" cried the fifteen little Hopkins.

Mr. and Mrs. Hopkins had the finest and most beautiful vegetable and flower gardens in all of Fiddle-Dee-Dee Farms.

Every spring, they would dig up the earth and rake it smooth. Next they would make long straight rows and put in the seeds. Finally they would cover the seeds and water them.

"When can we begin?" shouted the Hopkins children.

"This morning," said Daddy Hopkins. "While Mommy and I go to the store to buy carrot seeds, you can all start on the small radish garden. Now, line up so I can tell you what to do."

"Willy, Wiley, Wally, Wendy and Winny, take the spades and start digging up the earth."

"Hurrah!" cried the quintuplets.

"Bunny, Bonny, Billy and Biff, you four can rake," said Mommy Hopkins.

"Hooray!" cried the quadruplets.

"Flossie, Frannie and Fuffie, you make the rows for the seeds," said Daddy.

"Goody!" cried the triplets.

"Skipper and Skeezer," said Mommy, "you..."

"We know, we know. Plant the seeds," cried the twins.

"And what do I do?" asked Petey.

"You get to water it!" the Hopkins all shouted.

"Now, everyone to work," said Mommy and Daddy.

The Hopkins children ran to the garden. They could almost taste the fat pink radishes. They started in—all at the same time.

"We're supposed to dig first," said Willy, Wiley, Wally, Wendy and Winny.

"Wait until we rake," said Bunny, Bonny, Billy and Biff.

"Don't plant those seeds yet!" shouted Flossie, Frannie and Fuffie.

"You're getting us all wet," cried Skipper and Skeezer.

"It's my JOB," said Petey.

"What a mess!" cried Daddy Hopkins, home from the store. "There are too many Hopkins!"

"Now, now," said Mommy. "Let's start again. Everyone sit down. All right, quintuplets—DIG—"

Willy, Wiley, Wally, Wendy and Winny dug.

"Next—quadruplets—rake."

Bunny, Bonny, Billy and Biff raked.

"Triplets—make the rows."

Flossie, Frannie and Fuffie made the rows.

"Twins—plant the seeds."

Skipper and Skeezer planted the seeds.

"Petey—turn on the hose!" Petey did. And the radish garden was ready to grow.

"You see," said Mommy Hopkins. "There are not too many Hopkins."

"You're right," said Daddy Hopkins. "There are not too many Hopkins when they are not all in the same place at the same time."

MATH CONNECTIONS

Adding
Multiplying
Time

CULTURAL CONNECTION

Native American Folktale

Why Coyote Isn't Blue

FROM *AND IT IS STILL THAT WAY*, LEGENDS TOLD BY ARIZONA INDIAN CHILDREN, WITH NOTES BY BYRD BAYLOR

This story about Coyote, also known as Trotting Coyote, Changing Coyote, and Trickster Coyote, is told by Noel Roubidoux of the Pima Tribe in Arizona.

Long before other people were made, Coyote was walking around on the earth. He saw two bluebirds swimming in a pond. They seemed to be singing a certain song he had not heard before.

"What are you doing?" he asked them.

"We are renewing our feathers. We are keeping them blue."

Coyote wanted to be blue too. He asked them if he could make himself blue the way they did.

The birds told him the way to do it. "You swim in this pond four times every morning for four days. And every morning you sing this certain magic song."

"Teach me the song," Coyote said.

The bluebirds taught Coyote the song but they warned him that everything had to be done in the proper order to make it work.

Of course Coyote didn't listen to them. After he knew the song very well he jumped into the water and swam to the other side. He only did it once. He climbed out.

His brown fur was already blue and that made him very happy. He did not wait for the four days to pass. He just started singing the song as he ran off across the hills.

The birds saw that he was not following the rules of the color-changing ceremony. They flew after him at first and tried to get him to come back and swim four times.

Coyote didn't listen to them. He was already blue so he didn't care what they said. He was so proud of himself that he wanted all the animals to see him, so he sang louder and louder as he ran along.

Since there was no one else to see him, he kept looking at himself. He was not watching the path at all, just admiring his blue fur. He tripped over a rock and fell to the ground and rolled over and over in the soft dirt.

When Coyote got up again his fur was the color of dirt . . . just like it is today. If only Coyote had listened to the birds he would be blue today.

Noel Roubidoux
Pima
St. John's School

119

Band-Aids

FROM *WHERE THE SIDEWALK ENDS*
BY SHEL SILVERSTEIN

Can 70 Band-Aids fit on one small body? In Shel Silverstein's poem, 35 Band-Aids are already in place, and another box of 35 Band-Aids is standing by!

I have a Band-Aid on my finger,
One on my knee, and one on my nose,
One on my heel, and two on my shoulder,
Three on my elbow, and nine on my toes.
Two on my wrist, and one on my ankle,
One on my chin, and one on my thigh,
Four on my belly, and five on my bottom,
One on my forehead, and one on my eye.
One on my neck, and in case I might need 'em
I have a box full of thirty-five more.
But oh! I do think it's sort of a pity
I don't have a cut or a sore!

MATH CONNECTIONS

Adding
Subtracting
Number Sense
Estimating
Measuring

The Marrog

BY R. C. SCRIVEN

Creatures from Mars need more than 2 eyes and 2 ears and 10 fingers and 10 toes. Let children recast themselves as the Marrog and then find the sum of their digits as an exercise in adding 2-digit numbers.

My desk's at the back of the class
 And nobody, nobody knows
  I'm a Marrog from Mars
With a body of brass
 And seventeen fingers and toes.

Wouldn't they shriek if they knew
 I've three eyes at the back of my head
 And my hair is bright purple
My nose is deep blue
 And my teeth are half-yellow, half-red.

My five arms are silver, and spiked
 With knives on them sharper than spears.
I could go back right now if I liked—
 And return in a million light-years.

I could gobble them all
For I'm seven foot tall
 And I'm breathing green flames from my ears.

Wouldn't they yell if they knew,
    If they guessed that a Marrog was here?
Ha-ha, they haven't a clue—
      Or wouldn't they tremble with fear!
"Look, look, a Marrog"
    They'd all scream—and SMACK
The blackboard would fall and the ceiling would crack
    And teacher would faint, I suppose.
But I grin to myself, sitting right at the back
    And nobody, nobody knows.

MATH CONNECTIONS

Number Sense
Counting
Multiplying
Estimating

CULTURAL CONNECTION

West African Folktale

Leopard Finds Gold

RETOLD BY MARY PAT CHAMPEAU

The following is a folktale which is popular among the Hausa people of Niger in West Africa. Most folktales in Niger are not written down, but are passed from one generation to another through story telling.

Many, many years ago in the jungles of West Africa, there was a drought. Month after month, season after season, no rain fell from the sky. It was so hot during the day that the animals in the jungle could do nothing but sleep. After the sun went down, they would wake up and go out in the dark to look for water. Most of the lakes and streams had long since dried up, but there were still a few watering holes where a thirsty zebra or monkey or lion could get a cool drink.

One night, Leopard arrived at the watering hole to find many of his friends gathered around, not drinking the water, but staring into it and chattering excitedly.

"What's going on?" Leopard asked. "Is there food? Has someone found a fish?"

All of the animals turned to him. "No," said Elephant. "It's much better than that. Look!"

"What could possibly be better than food to a Leopard who's been hungry for a year?" asked Leopard.

"Come see for yourself," hissed Snake, dangling from his tree.

Leopard stepped up to the watering hole and saw at once what all the excitement was about.

"Why, it's gold!" he exclaimed, peering at the water in disbelief. Shimmering at the bottom of the pond were golden coins—more coins than Leopard could count. His mind began to work at once. Leopard was the greediest animal in the jungle. He wanted to have these coins all to himself—but how?

"Where did they come from?" he asked.

"We don't know," Giraffe answered. She stretched her long skinny neck in Leopard's direction. "Maybe they're part of a buried treasure."

It doesn't matter where they came from," said Rat impatiently. "That's not the point. The point is—how are we going to get them out of the pond?"

Leopard knew he had to think fast. Although the pond wasn't as deep as a lake, it was still too deep for him. He wasn't a good swimmer at all. But Elephant surely could reach the coins with her trunk if she wanted to, or Giraffe with her neck, or even Snake, if he coiled himself tightly to a low branch.

"Wait," said Leopard. "Before we try to get the coins out, I think we should count them."

"Count them?" said Hyena. "I can barely see them." Hyena was getting old and his eyes had begun to fail him.

"Why should we count them?" said Rat, even more impatient than before. "That's a silly idea."

"What's the matter?" asked Leopard, stalling for time in order to come up with a plan. "Don't you know how to count?"

Rat rolled his eyes. "Of course I know how to count. I have ten babies. I count them every day to be sure they're all safe." Rat stuck his pointy nose close to the water for a minute and then shook his whiskers dry. "All right, I've counted the coins. There are more than ten."

"How do you know you really counted them?" asked Leopard.

"One-two-three-four-five-six-seven-eight-nine-ten. And then some more." Rat counted out loud. "You see? More than ten."

"But that doesn't tell us how many there are altogether, does it?" asked Leopard.

"Who cares? Let's just get them out. I have ten hungry mouths to feed."

"Exactly why counting them is so important," said Leopard, his eyes shining. "We want to divide the coins evenly among us. If we know exactly how many coins there are, we will know how many each of us should get and there will be no fighting later on."

At this point, Monkey, sitting in his tree, suddenly became interested. He had been up above the other animals, eating a dried-up coconut and listening with half an ear to their silly talk. Now he climbed out quietly on the branch in order to hear more clearly. He had known Leopard for a very long time. Leopard never wanted to share anything.

"Leopard's right," said Elephant. "Let's be fair. I'll count the coins." She began to count. "One-two-three-four-five. There, it's settled."

Rat looked at Elephant in amazement. "What kind of counting is that?"

"It's counting to five. I don't know what comes after five. But I've counted all the coins, which you did not. I counted three fives. There are three-five coins."

"That's not a number," Hyena said. "I may not be able to see, but I know that three-five is not a number."

Leopard was delighted with the counting game. It was giving him time to think. A secret plan was brewing in his head.

Suddenly Zebra spoke up. "I've got it. Rat—you count the coins on your side of the watering hole and I'll count the coins on mine."

"All right," said Rat. "Anything to get this over with." He began, "One-two-three. . ." and, listening to Rat, Zebra remembered that she didn't know how to count. She had never learned. When Rat announced that there were ten coins on his side, Zebra said that there were ten coins on her side, too.

"How many is that?" asked Giraffe. "Ten coins on one side and ten on the other?"

"How should I know," said Zebra, blushing. "Ten and ten is. . .well, it's ten-ten!"

"That's not a number," Hyena said. "I may not be able to see very well, but I know that ten-ten is not a number." Zebra blushed again.

"You're red where you should be white, Zebra," said Elephant. "I don't think you can count at all."

"Let's not argue," said Snake.

"Snake's right," said Leopard. Snake looked at Leopard in surprise. They had never agreed on anything before. Leopard continued: "We mustn't argue. You are all to weak to argue. You're hungry and tired. It's been the longest dry season that any of us can remember. I am the only one who has been able to keep up his strength and therefore, I'll tell you what I'm going to do for you."

The animals listened intently. They didn't know that Leopard had hatched his secret plan and was hoping to trick them out of their coins.

"I want you to go home and get a good night's sleep," he told the animals. "Counting is very tiring work. It shouldn't be done late at night when we can hardly think straight. In the morning, when we are all refreshed, we'll meet back here and count the coins in daylight and divide them fairly among us."

"But what if someone else finds them while we're sleeping?" asked Elephant.

"Nobody will find them," said Leopard. "And do you know why? Because I am going to guard them. While you're sleeping, I'll stay awake and make sure that nobody comes and takes what is rightfully ours."

"I'll stay, too," said Rat, with a suspicious eye on Leopard. "I don't think you should have to guard the coins alone. It could be dangerous." The truth was, Rat didn't trust Leopard one bit.

"Don't be silly, Rat," Leopard retorted. "We'll need you bright-eyed and bushy-tailed in the morning. You are the only one who can count to ten." The other animals nodded.

"I don't know. . ." said Rat. But the animals convinced Rat that Leopard was right, and that he should go home and get some sleep with the rest of them.

In his mind, Leopard was already imagining how he would spend his coins. His plan was complete. As soon as the other animals were gone, he would set about gathering banana leaves. From these leaves he would make a strong net, attach the net to a long stick, and scoop up every single coin he could see. It was a wonderful, fool-proof plan and Leopard was very proud of himself for having thought it up. By the time the animals returned in the morning, he would be so far away there wouldn't be a chance of finding him.

"Thank you, Leopard," said Elephant. "I guess I've misjudged you all these years."

"Yes," added Giraffe. "Me, too. You're much kinder than I thought."

"Think nothing of it," said Leopard. "Now go on home and I'll see you in the morning."

And with that, all of the animals left the watering hole and went home to get a good night's sleep.

Leopard set to work at once. It didn't take him long at all to weave the net and find a long, sturdy stick. Just as he was about to dip his net into the water, he heard a voice calling to him from the tree.

"My friend," said Monkey. "What are you doing down there?"

"I'm no friend of yours," said Leopard. "Leave me alone. I'm fishing."

"Fishing?" said Monkey. "Is that so? You'll never catch anything that way." Monkey swung down to the lowest branch of his tree. "Your stick isn't long enough. Can't you swim?"

"Of course I can swim," said Leopard.

"You can swim as well as Zebra can count," Monkey thought to himself, but he didn't say anything.

"Why did you ask me if I could swim?" Leopard said.

"Because I've lived in this tree all my life and I've never seen anyone catch anything in that pond without getting wet."

Now Leopard was really confused. Everyone knew that Monkey was the smartest animal in the jungle, and it was true that Monkey had lived all his life in that tree. Perhaps he should listen to Monkey just this once. He thought of all those beautiful gold coins and how he had to have them. He put one paw into the water, then another, then another, and pretty soon he was up to his neck in the pond, splashing around and trying to get out to the middle.

"Well, well," Monkey laughed. "I don't think I've ever seen a Leopard swim before! And for what? Fishing in a pond with no fish!"

"I don't care about fish, you foolish Monkey," Leopard said, trying to manage his stick and net. "There are gold coins on the bottom of the pond and I'm going to get each and every one of them!"

Monkey shook his head. "Oh, my dear, wet friend. Wait for a moment and see what becomes of your gold coins."

A huge, dark cloud was rolling across the sky toward them.

"What are you talking about?" shouted Leopard. No sooner had he said these words than the cloud filled the sky above them and all of the coins disappeared.

Leopard blinked—he couldn't believe his eyes! "What? Monkey, what have you done? Where are my coins? My beautiful gold coins—they've vanished!"

But Monkey was laughing so hard he had to hold his sides to keep them from splitting. "I have never seen anything so funny in all my life," he said. "A Leopard who can't swim splashing around in the middle of a pond at night, trying to catch stars in a banana leaf basket!"

And sure enough, Leopard soon realized that Monkey was right. His gold coins were no more than the reflections of the stars twinkling in the water. "Oh no," Leopard moaned. "And I thought I would trick the other animals. I'm the one who's been tricked! What will they say in the morning when they come back? They'll never believe me!" He felt like sinking to the bottom of the pond.

"My friend," Monkey said. "Come out and dry yourself. Believe me when I tell you that there is not an animal in the jungle who will care about those gold coins in the morning."

Monkey looked up at the huge, dark cloud that hid the stars. He knew what that cloud meant. It meant that soon the jungle would be alive again and that the animals would be awake, singing and dancing for joy. Monkey climbed happily to the very top of his tree. He had already felt the first few drops of rain.

126

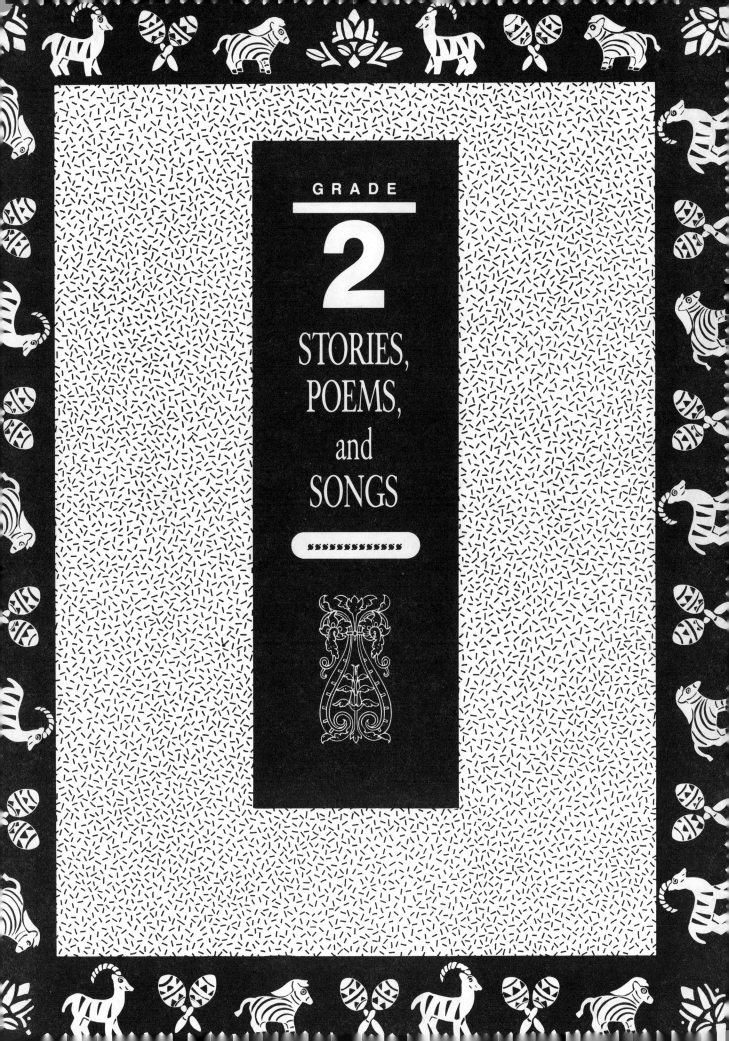

GRADE

2

STORIES, POEMS, and SONGS

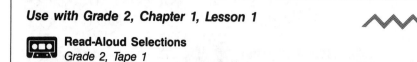

Use with Grade 2, Chapter 1, Lesson 1

🔲 **Read-Aloud Selections**
Grade 2, Tape 1
Side 1, Selection 1

MATH CONNECTIONS
Adding
Subtracting
Counting

CULTURAL CONNECTION
Haitian Story

The Banza

BY DIANE WOLKSTEIN

Can a banza *— a little banjo — protect a little goat named Cabree from 10 hungry tigers?
After Cabree plays a song on the banza, the tigers wonder if they can protect themselves
from a little goat!*

On the island of Haiti there once lived a little tiger named Teegra and a little goat named Cabree. Usually tigers and goats are enemies, but these two were best friends.

They had met during a thunderstorm when they had each run into the same cave for shelter. The storm had lasted all night, and when they came out in the morning, everything seemed strange to them, for they had come out of the cave by a different entrance and were lost.

They were both quite small, lonely, and afraid.

They looked at each other.

Cabree brayed, "Be-be. . . ."

Teegra roared, "Rrr. . . ."

"Do you want to be friends?" Cabree asked.

"Now!" Teegra answered.

So they wandered over the countryside, playing together, sharing whatever food they found, and sleeping close to each other at night for warmth.

Then one morning they found themselves in front of the cave where they had first met.

"rrRRRRR!"

Cabree turned. But it was not Teegra who had roared.

"RRRRRRrrr-rrRR!"

It was a roar of another tiger.

"Mama! Papa! *Auntie!*" Teegra cried joyfully as three huge tigers bounded out of the bushes.

Cabree ran into the cave without waiting.

After a while Teegra went to find Cabree, but Cabree refused to come out of the cave, so Teegra went home with his family.

The next morning Teegra went to the cave alone.

"Cabree!" he called. "I brought you a banza."

Cabree poked her head out of the cave.

"A *ban-za?* What's that?"

"A little banjo," Teegra said. "It belonged to my uncle, but I want you to have it—so it will protect you."

"How will the banza protect me?" Cabree asked.

"Auntie says, 'The banza belongs to the heart, and there is no stronger protection than the heart.' When you play the banza, Auntie says to place it over your heart, and 'one day the heart and banza will be one.'"

"Is that true?"

"Oh, Cabree, I don't really know, but I know I shall not forget you."

Teegra placed the banza around his friend's neck, then he turned to go.

"Where are you going?" Cabree asked.

"Home!" Teegra answered, and the little tiger ran back to his family without stopping.

Cabree stepped out of the cave so she could see the banza more clearly. It was a beautiful banza, and when the sun shone on it, it gleamed. Cabree held the banza over her heart. She stroked it gently. A friendly, happy sound came out. She stroked it again—and again—and before she realized it, she was trotting through the forest, humming to herself and stopping now and then to play a tune on the banza.

One afternoon Cabree came to a spring. She wanted to drink, but she was afraid the banza would get wet, so she took it off and carefully laid it down in the bushes. As she drank the cool sweet water she heard a low growl behind her.

"rrrRRrrr. . ."

Turning quickly, Cabree saw four large hungry tigers. Cabree wanted to leap across the stream and run away, but the banza was in the bushes behind the tigers. No! She would not leave the banza Teegra had given her.

Slowly and fiercely Cabree walked toward the banza.

Another tiger appeared. Now there were five.

Cabree kept walking.

"Where are you going?" the leader shouted.

Cabree reached the bushes. She picked up the banza and hung it around her neck. Then she turned to the tigers. Five more jumped out of the bushes.

Now there were ten!

"What have you put around your neck?" asked the leader.

And Cabree, trying to quiet her thundering, pounding heart, brought her foreleg to her chest and, by mistake, plucked the banza.

"A musician!" said the chief, laughing. "So you wish to play us a song?"

"No!" said Cabree.

"No?" echoed the leader. And all the tigers took a step closer to Cabree.

Teegra! Cabree wanted to shout. But Teegra was far away, and she was alone, surrounded by the tigers. No, she was not completely alone. She still had the banza Teegra had given her.

Cabree's heart beat very fast, but in time to her heartbeat she stroked the banza. She opened her mouth, and a song came out. To her own surprise it was a loud, low, ferocious song:

> Ten fat tigers, ten fat tigers,
> Cabree eats tigers raw.
> Yesterday Cabree ate ten tigers;
> Today Cabree eats ten more.

The tigers were astonished.

"Who is Cabree? And where did you learn that song?" demanded the chief.

"I am Cabree." Cabree answered in a new deep voice, and noticing how frightened the tigers looked, she added, "And that is *my* song. I always sing it before dinner."

The tiger chief realized that three of his tigers had suddenly disappeared.

"Madame Cabree," he said, "you play beautifully. Permit me to offer you a drink."

"Very well," said Cabree.

"Bring Madame Cabree a drink!" he ordered the two tigers closest to him, and as they started to leave he whispered, "and don't come back."

Five tigers stared at Madame Cabree.

Cabree stared back. Then she stroked her banza and sang, a little slower, but just as intently:

> Five fat tigers, five fat tigers,
> Cabree eats tigers raw.
> Yesterday Cabree ate ten tigers;
> Today Cabree eats five more.

"Oh! Oh-h-h! Something dreadful must have happened to my tigers," said the leader. "You." He motioned to the two tigers nearest him. "Go fetch Madame Cabree a drink." And again he whispered, "And don't come back."

Now only three tigers quaked before Madame Cabree. Cabree sang again:

> Three fat tigers, three fat tigers,
> Cabree eats tigers raw.
> Yesterday Cabree ate ten tigers;
> Today Cabree eats three more.

When she finished her song, only the leader remained. Cabree began:

> One fat tiger—

"Please," whispered the leader, "please let me go. I promise no tiger will ever bother you again."

Cabree looked at the trembling tiger. All she had done was to play the banza and sing what was in her heart. So Teegra's Auntie was right. Her heart had protected her. Her heart and her banza.

"Please!" begged the leader. "I'll do whatever you wish."

"Then go at once to Teegra, the little tiger who lives near the cave. Tell Teegra: 'Today Cabree's heart and the banza are one.' "

"Yes, yes," said the tiger. " 'Today Cabree's heart and the banza are one.' " And the tiger chief ran off to find Teegra.

With her banza gleaming around her neck, Cabree went trotting through the forest. But every now and then she would stop. She would stroke her banza and sing, for her heart would have a new song.

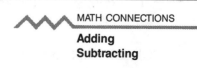
There Was an Old Man with a Beard

BY EDWARD LEAR

By finding out how many birds have made their nests in the old man's beard, children can explore facts to 8 and adding three numbers.

There was an Old Man with a beard,
Who said, "It is just as I feared! —
Two Owls and a Hen, four Larks and a Wren,
Have all built their nests in my beard!"

132

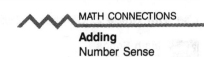
There Was an Old Man Who Said

BY ANONYMOUS

This poem can be used to encourage children to show how they would add 2 + 2. You may also want to substitute different numbers and create new addition facts.

There was an old man who said, "Do
Tell me *how* I should add two and two?
I think more and more
That it makes about four—
But I fear that is almost too few."

2+2

Use with Grade 2, Chapter 1, Lesson 4

Math Songs
Side 2, Selection 7

MATH CONNECTIONS

Adding
Subtracting
Counting

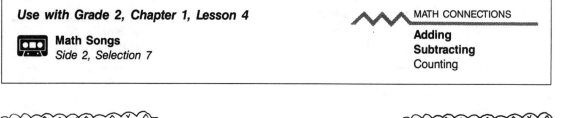

Five Fat Turkeys

In this traditional song, five fat turkeys avoid the cook by hiding in a tree. Let children use the song to make up their own addition and subtraction problems.

Traditional

Five fat tur-keys are we, _____

We slept all night in a tree. _____

When the cook came a-round we could-n't be found,

So that's why we're here, you see. _____

You can act out the song as you sing:

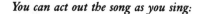

1. Hold up five separated fingers with the palm facing out.

2. Hold both hands in front of you, palm facing palm, with fingers slightly spread and curved; draw hands apart, larger than your body.

3. To represent the turkey's wattle, place the right hand at the chin and shake it back and forth.

4. Place both hands on the right cheek, bending the head slightly to the right.

5. Place the elbow of the right in the palm of the left hand. Shake the "Five" hand in and out several times.

6. Touch the thumb of the right hand to the lips and then move under the cupped left hand. (Use during last two lines of song "When the cook...you see.")

134

Use with Grade 2, Chapter 2, Lesson 1

 Read-Aloud Selections
Grade 2, Tape 1
Side 1, Selection 2

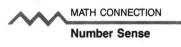 MATH CONNECTION

Number Sense

The Story Snail

BY ANNE ROCKWELL

The story snail gives John a hundred stories to tell, but after hearing the stories told once, twice, three times, everyone tires of them. John's own stories begin when he goes in search of the story snail for more tales to tell.

Chapter One

Once long ago there was a boy named John. John was good and kind but he could not do anything well. Nothing at all. And everyone laughed at him.

So one day he ran away. He ran away to the meadow and hid in the tall grass.

"Pssssst!" said a little voice.

John looked everywhere but he could not see anyone.

"Here I am," said the little voice. A snail with a silver shell was sitting on his shoe.

"I am a magic snail," it said. "I am the story snail. Because you cannot do anything well but are good and kind, I will give you a gift. I will give you one hundred stories no one has ever heard before. And whenever you tell a story, everyone will listen. 'How well he tells stories!' everyone will say."

And the snail told John one hundred stories. Then it crawled away.

Chapter Two

John went home. He told the first story just the way the snail had told it to him.

"That is a good story!" everyone said. "Tell us another story, John."

And John told another story.

Every day John told a story. He told stories until he had told every story the snail had given him.

135

"Tell the stories again!" the boys and girls said.

And John told the stories again

and again

and again —

until one day a little girl said, "Oh, tell us a new story. I have heard that story before."

"I do not know a new story," said John sadly.

And everyone laughed and said, "John tells the same stories over and over again. They are boring."

"I must go and find that magic snail and ask it for a new story," John said to himself.

He went back to the meadow. But the snail wasn't there.

Chapter Three

John called to the snail but it did not answer. He did not know what to do.

"Whoooooooo, wheeeeeeeee," he heard suddenly. "I am the Wild West Wind. The snail is far away. You will never, never find it. You had better go home. Whooooooo, wheeeeeeee."

And the Wild West Wind blew John's hat away.

But John would not go home. He walked and walked until he came to a dark forest.

In the forest John saw a green elf. "Have you seen a snail with a silver shell?" he asked.

"Once I saw that snail," the elf said, "but I do not know where it is now. It gave me one thousand stories. But because I did not tell them to anyone, they all turned to mushrooms!"

"Mushrooms?" said John.

"Yes, mushrooms," said the elf sadly. "All the mushrooms growing in this dark forest are the stories I did not tell. And the snail has never come back again. I can't tell you where he is," said the elf, "but I will give you a magic password. You never can tell, it may come in handy."

And he whispered to John, "Fuzzbuzzoncetherewas."

Chapter Four

John walked on until he came to the blue sea. He saw a mermaid sitting on a rock.

"Have you seen a snail with a silver shell? Do you know where it is?" John asked.

"No," said the mermaid. "But I can tell you what the seahorse told me. He has seen the snail with the silver shell."

"Tell me, please tell me!" said John.

"You must do a kind thing and a brave thing, and you must have a magic password. Then you will find the snail with the silver shell. That is what the seahorse told me."

"I have a magic password," said John "The elf gave it to me. If you tell me what to do I will do it."

But the mermaid swam away.

John walked on. He came to a garden. A little rabbit was sitting in the garden. It looked sad.

"Have you seen the snail with the silver shell? Do you know where it is?" said John.

"How would I know where it is? I do not even know where I am. I am lost," said the rabbit. And it began to cry.

"Don't cry," said John. "I will try to take you home. Where do you live?"

The little rabbit said, "I live at the edge of a dark forest. It is where the green elf lives. A thousand mushrooms grow there. It is far away."

"Poor me," thought John. "I have come so far, and now I must go backward. I will never find the snail now."

But he picked up the lost rabbit and patted its fur. "I will take you home," said John. "I have just come from that forest. I know where it is."

And he took the little rabbit home to its mother.

"You have done a very kind thing," said the mother rabbit and she gave John a carrot.

"Have you seen the snail with the silver shell? Do you know where it is?" said John.

"I have never seen it, but I have heard it from inside my rabbit hole," said the mother rabbit.

She pointed to a big rock and said, "Behind that rock there is a cave, and in that cave lives the snail with the silver shell."

"What have you heard?" said John.

"I have heard words, words, words," said the mother rabbit. "Have some lettuce."

But John ran to the rock.

Chapter Five

*J*ohn pushed the rock away. Something was growling in the deep, dark cave.

"That is not the snail with the silver shell," thought John.

He was afraid, but he went into the cave. He saw a bright red fire. Then he saw a big green dragon.

"Grrrrrr!" said the dragon. "Who are you? I do not like the looks of you. I might as well eat you up!"

"Please don't," said John. "I am John, and I have come to find the snail with the silver shell."

"I know that snail," said the dragon. "It lives in this cave with me, but it will not tell me any stories. It says I spit fire and growl and eat things up. I will not let you find it."

And the dragon growled.

"If I tell you a story," said John, "will you let me see the snail?"

"No!" said the dragon and he growled again.

"Two stories?" said John.

"No!" said the dragon and spit fire.

"Ten?" said John.

"One hundred!" shouted the dragon.

And so John told the dragon all the stories the snail had given him. And the dragon did not spit fire or eat John up. The dragon growled softly as he listened.

When John had told the last story, the dragon said, "Walk ten steps forward. Take twenty jumps to the right. Take one giant step backward. Close your eyes and jump up three times. Open your eyes and you will see a golden door. Knock once loudly and twice softly. Then say the magic password."

"And what is that?" said John.

"I do not know," said the dragon sadly. "The snail will not tell me."

But John knew.

Chapter Six

John walked ten steps forward and took twenty jumps to the right. He took one giant step backward, closed his eyes, and jumped up three times.

When he opened his eyes he saw a golden door. He knocked once loudly and twice softly. Then he said, "Fuzzbuzzoncetherewas!"

The golden door opened, and John saw the snail with the silver shell. It was eating a green leaf.

"Hello, snail," said John. "I have come to ask you for a new story. I have told all the stories you gave me. Even the dragon has heard them. No one wants to hear them again."

The snail stopped eating. It looked at John and poked out its little horns.

"I cannot give you a new story," the snail said. "There are many new stories to tell, that is true. But now you must find them for yourself. You have come so far, though, that I will send you safely home."

Softly the snail whispered, "Fuzzbuzzoncetherewas!" and John fell asleep at once.

Chapter Seven

*W*hen John woke up he was home.

"Have you found a new story, John?" everybody asked.

But John had no new story to tell.

Then he heard a bee buzz. Suddenly John smiled.

He said, "Fuzzbuzzoncetherewas a boy named John. John was good and kind but he could not do anything well. Nothing at all. And everyone laughed at him. So one day he ran away."

And John told about the magic snail with the silver shell, the story snail. He told about the Wild West Wind and the green elf. He told about the mermaid and the lost rabbit. He told about the dragon in the deep, dark cave. John told the story you have just read.

And after that, whenever he wanted, John told a new story.

And everyone said, "John tells stories very well indeed!"

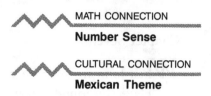

MATH CONNECTION
Number Sense

CULTURAL CONNECTION
Mexican Theme

A Birthday Basket for Tía

BY PAT MORA

Cecilia's great aunt, Tía, is almost 90 years old, and Cecilia wants to make the birthday a special day.

Today is secret day. I curl my cat into my arms and say, "Shsh, Chica. Today is secret day. Can you keep our secret, silly cat?"

Today is birthday day. Today is my great-aunt's ninetieth birthday. Ten, twenty, thirty, forty, fifty, sixty, seventy, eighty, ninety. Ninety years old. *Noventa años.*

At breakfast Mamá says, "What is today, Cecilia?"
I say, "Secret day. Birthday day."

Mamá cuts fruit for the surprise party. I sit in the backyard and watch Chica chase butterflies. I hear bees bzzzzzzz.

I draw pictures in the sand with a stick. I draw a picture of Tía, my aunt. I say, "Chica, what will we give Tía?"

Chica and I walk around the front yard and the backyard looking for a good present. We walk around the house. We look in closets and drawers.

I say, "Mamá, can Chica and I use this basket?" Mamá says, "Why, Cecilia?"
I say, "It's a surprise for the surprise party."

Chica jumps into the basket. "No," I say. "Not you, silly cat. This is a birthday basket for Tía."

I put a book at the bottom of the basket.
When Tía comes to our house, she reads to me. I sit close to her on the sofa. Sometimes Chica sits on the book. I say, "Silly cat. Books are not for sitting."

I put Tía's favorite mixing bowl on the book in the basket.
Tía and I like to make Mexican cookies for the family. Tía says, "Cecilia, help me stir the cookie dough." Tía says, "Cecilia, help me roll the cookie dough." Tía says, "Cecilia, you are a very good cook."

I put a flower pot in the mixing bowl on the book in the basket.
Tía and I grow flowers for the kitchen window. Chica likes to put her face in the flowers. I say, "Silly cat."

I put a teacup in the flower pot that is in the mixing bowl on the book in the basket.
When I'm sick, my aunt makes me hot mint tea, *hierbabuena*. She brings it to me in bed. She brings me a cookie too.

I put a red ball in the teacup that is in the flowerpot in the mixing bowl on the book in the basket.
On warm days Tía sits outside and throws me the ball. She says, "Cecilia, when I was a little girl in Mexico, my sisters and I played ball. We wore long dresses and had long braids."

Chica and I go outside. I pick flowers to decorate Tía's basket. On summer days when I swing, Tía collects flowers for my room.

Mamá says, "Cecilia, where are you?"

Chica and I run and hide our surprise.

I say, "Mamá, can you find the birthday basket for Tía?"

Mamá looks under the table. She looks in the refrigerator. She looks under my bed. She asks, "Chica, where is the birthday basket?"

Chica rubs against my closet door. Mamá and I begin to laugh. I show her my surprise.

After my nap, Mamá and I fill the piñata with fruit and candy. We fill the living room with balloons. I hum, "MMMMM" a little work song like Tía hums when she works. I help Mamá set the table with flowers and cakes.

"Here come the musicians," says Mamá. I open the front door. Our family and friends begin to arrive too.

I curl Chica into my arms. Then Mamá says, "Shsh, here comes Tía."

I rush to open the front door. "Tía! Tía!" I say. She hugs me and says, "Cecilia, what is this?"

"SURPRISE!" we all say. "*Feliz cumpleaños!* Happy birthday!"

"Tía! Tía!" I say. "It's secret day, birthday day! It's your ninetieth birthday surprise party!" Tía and I start to laugh.

I give her the birthday basket. She takes the red ball out of the teacup.
She takes the teacup out of the flowerpot.
She takes the flowerpot out of the bowl.
She takes the bowl off of the book.
She takes the book out of the basket.
And guess who jumps in the basket? Chica.
Everyone laughs.

Then the music starts and my aunt surprises me. She takes my hands in hers. Without her cane, she starts to dance with me.

MATH CONNECTIONS

Number Sense
Estimating
Time

CULTURAL CONNECTION

Chinese Folk Song

Song of the Dragon

The Chinese New Year, which lasts five days, is celebrated in this traditional Chinese folk song.

*Traditional Chinese
Folk Song*

See the drag-on come on a hun-dred legs!

He brings us all good cheer; him we do not fear!

Long life and peace and joy in the bright New Year!

(Instruments only)

New Year, New Year, New Year is here! _____

Homework Machine

FROM *A LIGHT IN THE ATTIC*
BY SHEL SILVERSTEIN

A homework machine sounds like a great idea — until it's put into operation. The machine doesn't add properly, but you'd never know it unless you knew your addition facts.

The Homework Machine, oh the Homework Machine,
Most perfect contraption that's ever been seen.
Just put in your homework, then drop in a dime,
Snap on the switch, and in ten seconds' time,
Your homework comes out, quick and clean as can be.
Here it is — "nine plus four?" and the answer is "three."
Three?
Oh me . . .
I guess it's not as perfect
As I thought it would be.

Use with Grade 2, Chapter 3, Lesson 5
Grade 2, Chapter 9, Lesson 3

MATH CONNECTIONS
Number Sense
Adding
Subtracting
Counting

CULTURAL CONNECTION
Japanese Story

A Thousand Pails of Water

BY RONALD ROY

To save a whale stranded on the beach, Yukio knows he must carry at least a thousand pails of water from the sea to keep the huge creature wet.

Yukio lived in a village where people fished and hunted whales to make their living. Yukio's father, too, was a whale hunter. "Why do you kill the whales, Father?" Yukio asked. "Suki's father works in the market and his hands are never red from blood."

"Hunting the whale is all I know," his father answered.

But Yukio did not understand.

Yukio went to his grandfather and asked again. "Why does my father kill the whales?"

"Your father does what he must do," his grandfather said. "Let him be, little one, and ask your questions of the sea."

So Yukio went to the sea.

Small creatures scurried from under his feet in the tide pools. Large scavenger birds screamed at him from the sky, "Bring us food!"

Then Yukio saw a whale that had become lodged between some rocks and was left behind when the tide went out.

The large tail flukes beat the sand, helplessly. The eye, as big as Yukio's hand, rolled in fright.

Yukio knew that the whale would not live long out of the sea. "I will help you, sir," he said.

But how? The whale was huge, like a temple.

Yukio raced to the water's edge. Was the tide coming in or going out? In, he decided, by the way the little fingers of foam climbed higher with each new wave.

The sun was hot on Yukio's back as he stood looking at the whale.

Yukio filled his pail with water and threw it over the great head.

"You are so big and my pail is so small!" he cried. "But I will throw a thousand pails of water over you before I stop."

The second pail went on the head as well, and the third and the fourth. But Yukio knew he must wet every part of the whale or it would die in the sun.

Yukio made many trips to the sea for water, counting as he went. He threw four pails on the body, then four on the tail, and then three on the head.

There was a little shade on one side of the big gray prisoner. Yukio sat there, out of breath, his heart pounding. Then he looked in the whale's eye and remembered his promise.

Yukio went back to the sea and stooped to fill his pail. How many had he filled so far? He had lost count. But he knew he must not stop.

Yukio fell, the precious water spilling from his pail. He cried, and his tears disappeared into the sand.

A wave touched his foot, as if to say, "Get up and carry more water. I am coming, but I am very slow."

Yukio filled his pail over and over. His back hurt, and his arms—but he threw and threw.

He fell again, but this time he did not get up.

Yukio felt himself being lifted.

"You have worked hard, little one. Now let us help."

Yukio's grandfather lay him in the shade of one of the rocks. Yukio watched his grandfather throw his first pail of water and go for another.

"Hurry!" Yukio wanted to scream, for his grandfather was old and walked slowly.

Then Yukio heard the voices. His father and the village people were running toward the sea. They carried pails and buckets and anything that would hold water.

Some of the villagers removed their jackets and soaked them in the sea. These they placed on the whale's burning skin. Soon the whale was wet all over.

Slowly the sea came closer and closer. At last it covered the huge tail. The village people ran back and forth carrying water, shouting to each other. Yukio knew the whale would be saved.

Yukio's father came and stood by him. "Thank you, Father," Yukio said, "for bringing the village people to help."

"You are strong and good," his father said. "But to save a whale many hands must carry the water."

Now the whale was moving with each new wave. Suddenly a great one lifted him free of the rocks. He was still for a moment, then, with a flip of his tail, swam out to sea.

The villagers watched silently, as the whale swam farther and farther from their shore. Then they turned and walked toward the village.

Except for Yukio, who was asleep in the arms of his father. He had carried a thousand pails of water, and he was tired.

MATH CONNECTIONS

Adding
Subtracting
Multiplying

Don't Ask Me

BY YOLANDA NAVE

Yolanda Nave has expressed how some children may feel about mathematics. Letting children create their own games may give you a better assessment of their work.

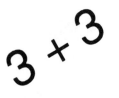

Don't ask *me*
What's three plus three;
Oh please don't call my name.
Please don't say
We're going to play
Another numbers game.

What's ten minus four?
Four minus two?
I do apologize. . . .
But to be exact,
When I subtract
I get butterflies.

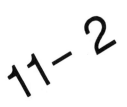

What's two from eleven?
One times seven?
I really cannot tell.
If you'll excuse me,
Numbers confuse me—
But I can spell very well.

Use with Grade 2, Chapter 4, Lesson 1

Read-Aloud Selections
Grade 2, Tape 1
Side 2, Selection 1

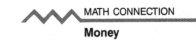
MATH CONNECTION
Money

Penelope Gets Wheels

BY ESTHER ALLEN PETERSON

It's Penelope's birthday, and she wants wheels (a bicycle, please). Although she doesn't have enough money to buy a bicycle, Penelope discovers the advantages of the wheels she can afford.

It was Penelope's birthday, and she got 10 one dollar bills, 4 quarters, and 5 dimes.

She counted the money many times, and it always came out the same: $11.50.

"I am rich and I am older now," she said to her mom. "I don't need to walk anymore. I will go on wheels."

"Wheels?" asked her mom.

"Yes," said Penelope. "I would like a car, but I know I am not rich enough or old enough. I think I will buy a bicycle."

"A bicycle costs a lot of money," said her mom.

"I have lots of money," Penelope said. And before her mother could say another word, she ran outside and went to the nearest department store.

"Today is my birthday," she said to the saleslady. "I would like to buy that silver racing bike."

"That bicycle costs one hundred and nineteen dollars," the saleslady said.

Penelope pointed to a smaller bike. "How much is that one?"

"Seventy-nine dollars and ninety-five cents," said the saleslady.

"I'm not that rich," Penelope said, and she put the money back in her pocket.

Penelope looked at badminton sets, paint-by-number kits, and baseball bats and gloves. But she didn't want to buy anything she saw.

Then she saw some roller skates. They were $9.95 a pair.

She picked up a skate and spun its wheels. "I guess these are all I can afford."

"That will be ten dollars and forty-five cents with tax," the saleslady said.

Penelope paid for the skates.

She went outside, put them on, and started skating home. She still wished she was old enough to drive a car or rich enough to own a bicycle.

When she got home her mom and dad were in the kitchen. "I didn't have enough money for a bicycle," she said. "All I could afford were roller skates."

"But roller skates are the best wheels a kid can have," said her dad.

Penelope shoved one of the skates across the floor. "Skating is better than walking, but I'd still rather have a bike."

The next day everyone was going to the ball park to see Slugger Jones hit his five-hundredth home run. Slugger Jones was Penelope's favorite ballplayer, and she was going, too.

As she sat on the steps putting on her roller skates, Mr. Smith came out of his house and got into his car.

"Are you going to the game?" Penelope asked.

"Sure am," answered Mr. Smith.

"I'm skating to the game," said Penelope.

"Be sure you don't get any speeding tickets," he said, and he drove off.

Penelope skated toward the ball park. Her friend Jim rode by on his bicycle.

"Going to the game?" she asked.

"Yep," he said.

"I am too," said Penelope.

"Let's race," said Jim.

Penelope skated as fast as she could, but Jim got ahead of her. Soon she couldn't see him at all.

Penelope skated fast for six blocks and then stopped. Cars were lined up waiting to get into the parking lot.

Penelope skated past Mr. Smith. "I didn't get any speeding tickets," she said.

"Really!" said Mr. Smith.

Near the entrance to the ball park Penelope saw Jim looking for a place to lock his bike. She skated past him. "Does the winner get a prize?"

Penelope took off her skates, strapped them together, and waited in line to buy her ticket.

Then she went straight to her favorite seat in the grandstand.

Soon everyone stood up and sang the national anthem. The umpire yelled, "PLAY BALL!"

Jim walked by looking for a seat.

During the second inning Mr. Smith came in.

Penelope giggled and said, "Roller skates are the best wheels a kid can have."

Hot Cross Buns

Children can investigate the prices of various other items after listening to this traditional song.

Traditional

Hot cross buns, hot cross buns, one-a-pen-ny, two-a-pen-ny, hot cross buns.

Use with Grade 2, Chapter 5, Lesson 1

 Read-Aloud Selections
Grade 2, Tape 1
Side 2, Selection 2

MATH CONNECTIONS

Measuring
Time
Estimating

How Big Is a Foot?

BY ROLF MYLLER

Rolf Myller's story points out the importance of standard units of measure.

Once upon a time there lived a King and his wife, the Queen. They were a happy couple for they had everything in the World.

However. . .when the Queen's birthday came near the King had a problem: What could he give to Someone who had Everything?

The King thought and he thought and he thought. Until suddenly, he had an idea! HE WOULD GIVE THE QUEEN A BED. The Queen did not have a bed because at the time beds had not been invented. So even Someone who had Everything—did not have a bed.

The King called his Prime Minister and asked him to please have a bed made.

The Prime Minister called the Chief Carpenter and asked him to please have a bed made.

The Chief Carpenter called the apprentice and told him to make a bed.

"How big is a bed?" asked the apprentice, who didn't know because at the time nobody had ever seen a bed.

"How big is a bed?" the Carpenter asked the Prime Minister.

"A good question," said the Prime Minister. And he asked the King, "HOW BIG *IS* A BED?

The King thought and he thought and he thought. Until suddenly he had an idea! THE BED MUST BE BIG ENOUGH TO FIT THE QUEEN.

The King called the Queen. He told her to put on her new pajamas and told her to lie on the floor.

The King took off his shoes and with his big feet walked carefully around the Queen. He counted that the bed must be THREE FEET WIDE AND SIX FEET LONG to be big enough to fit the Queen. (Including the crown which the Queen sometimes liked to wear to sleep.)

The King said "Thank you," to the Queen, and told the Prime Minister, who told the Chief Carpenter, who told the apprentice: "The bed must be three feet wide and six feet long to be big enough to fit the Queen." (Including the crown which she sometimes liked to wear to sleep.)

The apprentice said "Thank you," and took off his shoes, and with his little feet he measured three feet wide and six feet long and made a bed to fit the Queen.

When the King saw the bed, he thought it was beautiful. He could not wait for the Queen's Birthday. Instead, he called the Queen at once and told her to put on her new pajamas.

Then he brought out the bed and told the Queen to try it. BUT the bed was much too small for the Queen.

The King was so angry that he immediately called the Prime Minister who called the Chief Carpenter who called the jailer who threw the apprentice into jail.

The apprentice was unhappy. WHY WAS THE BED TOO SMALL FOR THE QUEEN?

He thought and he thought and he thought. Until suddenly he had an idea! A bed that was three King's feet wide and six King's feet long was naturally bigger than a bed that was three apprentice feet wide and six apprentice feet long.

"I CAN MAKE A BED TO FIT THE QUEEN IF I KNOW THE SIZE OF THE KING'S FOOT," he cried.

He explained this to the jailer, who explained it to the Chief Carpenter, who explained it to the Prime Minister, who explained it to the King, who was much too busy to go to the jail.

Instead, the King took off one shoe and called a famous sculptor. The sculptor made an exact marble copy of the King's foot. This was sent to the jail.

The apprentice took the marble copy of the King's foot, and with it he measured three feet wide and six feet long and built a bed to fit the Queen!

The Bed was ready just in time for the Queen's Birthday. The King called the Queen and told her to put on her new pajamas. Then he brought out the New Bed and told the Queen to try it. The Queen got into bed and...THE BED FIT THE QUEEN PERFECTLY. (Including the crown which she sometimes liked to wear to sleep.)

It was, without a doubt, the nicest gift that the Queen had ever received.

The King was very happy. He immediately called the apprentice from jail and made him a royal prince.

He ordered a big parade, and all the people came out to cheer the little apprentice prince.

And forever after, anyone who wanted to measure anything used a copy of the King's foot. And when someone said, "My bed is six feet long and three feet wide," everyone knew exactly how big it was.

A New Coat for Anna

BY HARRIET ZIEFERT

Anna needs a new coat, but because of the war, there are none in the stores. Her mother barters with various people to buy wool and then has it spun, dyed, and woven into a piece of cloth that the tailor can cut and sew into a beautiful coat.

Winter had come and Anna needed a new coat. The fuzzy blue coat that she had worn for so many winters was no longer fuzzy and it was very small.

Last winter Anna's mother had said, "When the war is over, we will be able to buy things again and I will get you a nice new coat."

But when the war ended the stores remained empty. There still were no coats. There was hardly any food. And no one had any money.

Anna's mother wondered how she could get Anna a new coat. Then she had an idea. "Anna, I have no money," she said, "but I still have Grandfather's gold watch and some other nice things. Maybe we can use them to get what we need for a new coat. First we need wool. Tomorrow we will visit a farmer and see about getting some."

The next day Anna and her mother walked to a nearby farm.

"Anna needs a new coat," Anna's mother told the farmer. "I have no money, but I will give you this fine gold watch if you will give me enough wool from your sheep to make a coat."

The farmer said, "What a good idea! But you will have to wait until spring when I shear my sheep's winter wool. Then I can trade you their wool for your gold watch."

Anna waited for spring to come. Almost every Sunday she and her mother visited the sheep. She would always ask them, "Is your wool growing?" The sheep would always answer, "Baaa!" Then she would feed them nice fresh hay and give them hugs.

At Christmastime Anna brought them paper necklaces and apples and sang carols.

When spring came the farmer sheared the sheep's wool.

"Does it hurt them?" asked Anna.

"No, Anna," said the farmer. "It is just like getting a haircut."

When he had enough wool to make a coat, the farmer showed Anna how to card the wool. "It's like untangling the knots in your hair," he told Anna.

Then he gave Anna's mother a big bag of wool and Anna's mother gave him the gold watch.

Anna and her mother took the bag of wool to an old woman who had a spinning wheel.

"Anna needs a new coat," Anna's mother told the woman. "I have no money, but I will give you this beautiful lamp if you will spin this wool into yarn."

The woman said, "A lamp. That's just what I need. But I cannot spin quickly, for I am old and my fingers are stiff. Come back when the cherries are ripe and I will have your yarn."

When summer came, Anna and her mother returned. Anna's mother gave the old woman the lamp and the old woman gave them the yarn—and a basket of delicious red cherries.

"Anna, what color coat would you like?" Anna's mother asked.

"A red one!" Anna answered.

"Then we will pick some lingonberries," said Anna's mother. "They make a beautiful red dye."

At the end of summer, Anna's mother knew just the place in the woods to find the ripest lingonberries.

Anna and her mother boiled water in a big pot and put the berries into it. The water turned a deep red. Anna's mother dipped the pale yarn into it.

Soon red yarn was hanging up to dry on a clothesline strung across the kitchen.

When it dried, Anna and her mother wound the yarn into balls.

They took the yarn to the weaver.

"Anna needs a new coat," Anna's mother said. "I have no money, but I will give you this garnet necklace if you will weave this yarn into cloth."

The weaver said, "What a pretty necklace. I will be happy to weave your yarn. Come back in two weeks."

When Anna and her mother returned, the weaver gave them a bolt of beautiful red cloth. Anna's mother gave the weaver the sparkling garnet necklace.

The next day Anna and her mother set off to see the tailor.

"Winter is coming and Anna needs a new coat," Anna's mother told the tailor. "I have no money, but I will give you this porcelain teapot if you will make a coat from this cloth."

The tailor said, "That's a pretty teapot. Anna, I'd be very happy to make you a new coat, but first I must take your measurements."

He measured her shoulders. He measured her arms. He measured from the back of her neck to the back of her knees. Then he said, "Come back next week and I will have your coat."

The tailor set to work making a pattern, cutting the cloth, pinning, and sewing and stitching and snipping. He worked and worked for almost a whole week. When he was finished, he found six pretty matching buttons in his button box and sewed them on the coat.

He hung the coat proudly in the window for everyone to see.

When Anna and her mother returned to the tailor's shop, Anna tried on her new coat. She twirled around in front of the mirror. The coat was perfect!

Anna thanked the tailor. Anna's mother thanked him, too, and gave him the pretty porcelain teapot.

Anna wore her new coat home. She stopped at every store to look at her reflection in the window.

When they got home her mother said, "Christmas will soon be here, and I think this year we could have a little celebration."

Anna said, "Oh, yes, and please could we invite all the people who helped to make my coat?"

"Yes," said Anna's mother. "And I will make a Christmas cake just like I used to."

Anna gave her mother a big hug.

On Christmas Eve the farmer, the spinner, the weaver, and the tailor came to Anna's house. They all thought Anna looked beautiful in her new coat.

The Christmas cake that Anna's mother baked was delicious. Everyone agreed that this was the best Christmas they had had in a long time.

On Christmas Day Anna visited the sheep. "Thank you for the wool, sheep," she said. "Do you like my pretty new coat?"

The sheep seemed to smile as they answered, "Baaa! Baaa!"

Use with Grade 2, Chapter 5, Lesson 6

Math Songs
Side 2, Selection 10

MATH CONNECTIONS
Measuring
Time
Estimating

CULTURAL CONNECTION
Chinese Folk Song

Spring in China

As the song illustrates, spring in China is the same as spring in our country. The snow melts, flowers begin to grow, and songbirds return. At about what temperature (in both degrees Fahrenheit and degrees Centigrade) do these things occur?

Chinese Folk Song

Spring brings the sun - shine to melt win - ter's snow.

Spring brings the warm rains to help flow - ers grow.

Spring brings song - birds from far a - way;

Joy - ful mu - sic is heard all day,

Min - gling with laugh - ter as chil - dren play.

157

Use with Grade 2, Chapter 6, Lesson 1

 Read-Aloud Selections
Grade 2, Tape 1
Side 2, Selection 3

MATH CONNECTIONS

Adding
Number Sense
Geometry

Ninety-Nine Pockets

BY JEAN MYRICK

For his birthday, Jeremy receives a suit with ninety-nine pockets sewn onto it. How many pockets would children in your class like to have? What would their suits look like?

"**J**eremy, what would you like for your birthday?"

Jeremy jumped up from the floor where he was reading the funnies and ran over to his mother's chair. He had been waiting for that question for days and he had his answer all ready. "I would like to have you make me a pocket suit!"

"A suit? But you have your best Sunday suit, and you have corduroys for school and jeans for play. Why do you want another suit?"

"This would be a *pocket* suit. It would have pockets all over it—long skinny ones for pencils and rulers and my pocket knife, a round one for my compass, a big, squarish one for a book, a little one with a button for money, a bag-shaped one for an apple, one for nails, and one for my hammer—or maybe that could hang from a little loop like the one on Uncle Ted's white coveralls."

Jeremy stopped long enough to get his breath. Then he continued, "I'll need a pocket for my flashlight, and pockets for my collections of bottlecaps and rocks—I don't suppose I could carry all of them, just a few of the special ones—and some extra pockets for things I might find. Oh, and pockets for string and glue and marbles, and one for my rope and my magnifying glass, and—and—Boy, could I have a hundred pockets, Mom? Could I?"

"My goodness!" exclaimed Mother. "Where would I ever get a pattern for a suit like that? You had better draw a picture for me."

So Jeremy got a pencil and a big piece of paper and started making a picture of his pocket suit.

It was bedtime before he finished, so he put the paper under his pillow, in case he thought of anything in the middle of the night.

All the next day Jeremy worked on his suit pattern. He kept thinking of more and more things he would like to carry with him. His mother asked him to take a note to Aunt Beatrice, so he drew a note pocket on his collar. Then he decided to have one on each side, so he could carry notes coming and going and not get mixed up. Left going, right coming.

Hiram, his hamster, looked so lonesome when Jeremy put him back in his cage that Jeremy dashed up to his room and added a hamster pocket on the back of his right shoulder.

Jeremy's mother went downtown and bought seven yards of blue denim—three yards for the suit and four yards for all of the pockets.

Jeremy started carrying around a little notebook to write down more pockets as he thought of them. He decided to have a yardstick pocket on his left trouser leg and a saw pocket on his right leg. His telescope could go on his left sleeve, and the periscope he had made out of a wax paper tube could go on his right sleeve. No, it had better be the other way around, so the periscope wouldn't get smashed. His lunch pocket would be, naturally, right over his stomach.

The evening before Jeremy's birthday his mother straightened up from her sewing, bit off her thread, and said, "Jeremy, I think your suit is finished. Every last pocket is stitched in place."

"Does it really have a hundred pockets?"

"I'm sorry, Jeremy, but it has only ninety-nine."

"Couldn't we make just one more so it would have a hundred?"

"Jeremy Jason Jones!" said his mother. "This suit has round pockets, triangular pockets, square pockets, long, thin pockets, baggy pockets! It has pockets on pockets, pockets inside of pockets, and pockets inside of pockets on pockets! There is not room for one more pocket! Besides, I don't have any more denim."

"O.K. Thanks, Mom. Boy, I bet even the President doesn't have a suit with ninety-nine pockets! Wait till I show the kids tomorrow! Oh boy! Ninety-nine pockets!"

Jeremy woke up early the next morning, he was so anxious to wear his new suit. It didn't take him long to get dressed *this* morning, but his mother called him to breakfast before he had more than eight pockets filled. He was just finishing his breakfast when Steve, Peter, and David stopped by for him. Jeremy ran upstairs while his mother went to answer the door.

"Ask them to wait a couple of minutes, and I'll show them something they've never seen before!" he called down the stairs. He hurried to put his police whistle, his squirt gun, his popsicle sticks, and his bubble gum funnies in the pockets designed for them.

"David says to hurry," Mother called up to him.

"Coming," Jeremy answered, and squeezed his bunch of keys, the chain from the bathtub plug, his oil can, his crayons, and his collapsible cup into their pockets.

"Hurry up, Jeremy," called Peter. "I have to be home by 11:30."

"I'm coming," yelled Jeremy, putting his notebook, his mouth organ, his magnet, and marbles in place.

"We're going on over to Mark's house. You come when you get ready," Steve called from the foot of the stairs.

"All right. I'll be there in a flash." Jeremy grabbed his little funnel, his camp shovel, his four big steel ball bearings, and the nutcracker and shoved them into their pockets. Now he just had to put in his rocks and spare batteries, and— OOOOPS! "Hey, Mom! Mother!"

His trousers had been sinking lower and lower on his hips. Now they dropped to the floor with a THUD! and a JANGLE! a CRASH! and a SMASH! and a SPLAT!

Mother and Father rushed upstairs in alarm. As they stood in the doorway staring at him, Jeremy felt that he had to say something. "I guess I need suspenders."

"Two pairs of suspenders—and a belt," Mother suggested.

"Or a portable derrick," added Father, smiling.

Jeremy could not move around very well with everything hanging around his ankles, so Mother found his old suspenders and then took the new ones from his Sunday suit. She finally added an old pair of Father's, which she shortened with safety pins. And then, somehow, she managed to buckle on two belts.

Jeremy found it a little difficult to bend down. "Would you mind handing me that file over there, please, Mother? And would you please slide that yardstick in this long pocket on my left leg, and the saw on the other side? Now my telescope goes on the right sleeve and the periscope on the left sleeve."

"Oh, oh!" said Father, laughing. "Do you think you can walk? Let's see you bend your arm."

Jeremy tried. He couldn't bend either his knees or his elbows!

"We forgot to put joints in this suit!" said Father. Jeremy finally agreed that he would have to get along with only his six-inch ruler for measuring and his pocket knife for cutting.

He was in a hurry to get over to Mark's house, so he decided to leave Hiram in his cage and not to take his shell collection along this time. Mother and Father insisted on helping him down the stairs, one on each side, holding an arm.

"Bye, Mom! Bye, Dad!" Jeremy shouted back as he started off for Mark's. "Thanks for helping me get ready. And thanks a million, Mother, for making my suit! I'll be ba—"

SPLASH! THUD! JANGLE! CRASH! SMASH! SPLAT! BOOM! and especially, OUCH! Jeremy's right side pockets with the rocks and ball bearings and the camp shovel and the nails had over-balanced the lighter left side and tumbled Jeremy into the big mud puddle he had made yesterday when he forgot to move the hose.

"Just look at that suit!" Mother cried, as soon as she was sure that Jeremy was not really hurt. "You take it off and put it in the wash this minute! And be sure you take every single thing out of the pockets!"

"But Mom, it will take me an hour to unload."

"I'll help you. Come up to your room, so we can put things away."

Mother and Father helped him up the stairs again, and Mother took out enough things so that Jeremy could move around to empty the rest.

"Mother," said Jeremy slowly, "I wouldn't want to hurt your feelings after you worked so hard, but do you think there could be such a thing as too many pockets?"

"It looks as though there might well be."

"How many pockets do you think a boy should have?"

"Well, I would say one on each side—"

"And maybe two in the back? Mom, do you know what? My jeans are just perfect. A pocket for each hand and two extra in the back. And I have two pockets in my shirt, besides. Six pockets ought to be enough for any boy, don't you think so, Mom?"

"But what shall we do with this suit? It took me so long to make it."

"I know!" said Jeremy, triumphantly. "I can hang it up on my coat-tree and store everything in its own pocket just as we planned. I guess I don't really need to carry everything around with me all the time. I bet I'll have the only hanging toy chest in the neighborhood!"

Use with Grade 2, Chapter 6, Lessons 6 and 7
Grade 2, Chapter 7, Lesson 3

MATH CONNECTIONS
Adding
Subtracting
Money

A Hot Thirsty Day

BY MARJORIE WEINMAN SHARMAT

Marjorie Weinman Sharmat's story demonstrates the importance of group decision making.

Tommy and Jon and Mitchell were sitting under a tree.

"Who has a dime?" asked Tommy.

Mitchell looked in Tommy's right pocket.

He looked in Tommy's left pocket.

He looked under Tommy's cap.

"You don't have a dime," he said.

"I know I don't," said Tommy. "That's why I asked for one."

"If I had a dime, I would have spent it," said Jon.

"I have three dimes," said Mitchell.

"You do?" said Tommy.

"Yes," said Mitchell. "They're in my piggy bank."

"Can you get them?" asked Jon.

"Sure," said Mitchell. "Nobody is home. The key is outside in the geranium pot. I'll go home, get the key and open the door. I'll get a ladder from the cellar and take it to my room. I'll climb the ladder to the top shelf of my closet and take my piggy bank down. I'll break the piggy bank with a hammer and take out the three dimes. Then I'll bring them here."

"Never mind," said Jon. "There must be an easier way to get money."

"I know," said Tommy. "Let's start a business."

"Good idea," said Mitchell. "How about a spy business?"

"You need a trench coat for that," said Jon. "Do you have a trench coat?"

"My father has one," said Mitchell. "But he isn't a spy. He's a milkman."

"Think of another business," said Tommy.

"I know," said Jon. "The chocolate ice cream business."

"Chocolate ice cream isn't a business," said Tommy. "You have to sell all the flavors."

"I only like chocolate," said Jon.

"Think some more," said Tommy.

"I can't think of anything as good as the chocolate ice cream business," said Jon.

"I know," said Mitchell. "The lemonade business."

"No," said Tommy.

"No," said Jon. "There are three lemonade stands on this block."

"Keep thinking," said Tommy.

They thought about the lawn-mowing business.

"Too hard," said Tommy.

They thought about the snow-shoveling business.

"No snow," said Jon.

"The lemonade business is a good business," said Mitchell.

"No," said Tommy.

"No," said Jon.

They thought about selling worms.

They thought about selling old toys.

And Mitchell thought about selling his geraniums.

Nothing seemed right.

"The lemonade business is a good business," said Mitchell.

Tommy looked at Jon. Jon looked at Tommy. They all walked to Tommy's house. They took some things from the refrigerator. They took some things from a shelf. They took some things from the cellar, the laundry room and a wastebasket.

They went back outside. The pasted, painted, hammered and pasted some more.

And they started the fourth lemonade stand on the block.

"I'm in charge of the lemons, sugar, water and ice," said Jon.

And I'm in charge of the money," said Tommy.

"The lemonade looks good," said Mitchell. "I think I'll be in charge of tasting it.

"No," said Tommy. "You're in charge of stirring. You stir the lemon juice, sugar, water and ice."

"All right," said Mitchell. "But I'm a better taster than stirrer."

"Here come three ladies," said Tommy. "Now stand straight and smile."

"Hello," said one of the ladies. "It's a nice day."

"Yes," said Mitchell. "It's a nice, thirsty, hot, thirsty day." And he stirred hard. The ice cubes clinked.

"A very nice day," said the other ladies. And they walked on.

"They didn't buy any lemonade," said Tommy.

Two men came along. Tommy and Jon stood straight and smiled. Mitchell stirred hard. The ice cubes clanked.

The men walked right by.

Tommy stopped smiling. "Business is terrible," he said.

"We can still sell my geraniums," said Mitchell.

"Maybe our lemonade costs too much," said Jon.

"Say, maybe you're right," said Tommy. "Let's find out how much it costs at the other stands on the block."

"Who'll go and find out?" asked Jon. He looked at Mitchell.

"I don't know," said Tommy. And he looked at Mitchell, too.

"I'll go," said Mitchell. "My arm is tired from stirring."

He ran down the street, Soon he came running back around the other end of the block.

"I was right," he said. "It's a nice, thirsty, hot, thirsty day. I need some lemonade."

"What did you find out?" asked Tommy.

"I found out that I don't need a trench coat to be a spy," said Mitchell. "They told me I was a spy."

"Did you find out what their lemonade costs?" asked Jon.

"Seven cents a glass," said Mitchell.

"Very good," said Tommy. "Our lemonade will cost less. Our lemonade will cost six cents a glass."

Some girls walked down the street. Mitchell stirred hard. But all the ice had melted.

"Look," said one of the girls. "Only six cents a glass for lemonade. It costs seven cents at the other stands."

The girls bought four glasses.

"Four glasses at six cents a glass," said Tommy. "We made twenty-four cents."

A woman with a cat came along. "One glass of lemonade, please," she said. She took a saucer from her pocketbook. She poured the lemonade into the saucer. "My cat loves lemonade," she said.

The cat lapped up all the lemonade in the saucer.

"Would you like some, too," asked Tommy.

"No," she said. "I only drink milk."

She picked up the empty saucer. She put it back in her pocketbook, picked up her cat and walked away.

"Another six cents," said Tommy. "Now we have twenty-four cents and six cents. That makes thirty cents."

"Here come three boys," said Jon.

Mitchell looked at the boys. Then he ducked behind the lemonade sign.

The boys walked up to the stand. "I'm Charlie," said one of them. "Some girls told us that you sell lemonade for six cents a glass."

"That's right," said Tommy. "Would you like some?"

"We *have* some," said Charlie. "We own the other lemonade stands on the block."

"You do?" said Tommy.

"Do you?" asked Jon.

Mitchell didn't say anything. He bent his head lower behind the sign.

"We sell lemonade for seven cents a glass," said Charlie. "You will spoil our business."

"We will?" said Tommy.

"Will we?" asked Jon.

Mitchell knocked over the sign.

"It's the spy!" said Charlie.

"Hello," said Mitchell. "Would you like to buy a geranium?"

"No," said Charlie. "We'd like to buy your lemonade business."

"You would?" said Tommy.

"You know we put a lot of lemon and sugar into this business," said Mitchell. He looked at his arm. "And a lot of stirring, too. The price is seventy-five cents."

"We'll pay you forty-five cents," said Charlie.

"We'll take it," said Mitchell.

Mitchell, Tommy and Jon counted their money. "We've got a lot more than a dime," said Jon. "What did you want a dime for, Tommy?"

"I forgot," said Tommy.

"Think," said Jon.

"A geranium costs about a dime," said Mitchell.

"No, it wasn't that," said Tommy.

"A chocolate ice cream?" said Jon.

"No, not that," said Tommy.

"I'm still thirsty," said Mitchell. "I think I'll buy some lemonade."

"That sounds good," said Tommy. "That sounds better than what I forgot. Let's all buy some."

And they did. Because it was a nice, thirsty, hot, thirsty day.

Use with Grade 2, Chapter 7, Lesson 1

 Read-Aloud Selections
Grade 2, Tape 2
Side 1, Selection 1

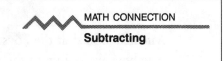 MATH CONNECTION
Subtracting

Using Subtraction

BY LEE BLAIR FROM *ARITHMETIC IN VERSE AND RHYME*

What would children in your class like to subtract from their lives?

I've often heard
the teacher say,
"Subtract means less,
or *take away*."
And so I'd get
great satisfaction
if I could only
do subtraction
on all of these—
yes, all of these:
    Liver,
    Spinach,
    "Quiet, please,"
    scoldings,
    early bedtime,
    rice,
    rainy Sundays,
    "Do be nice,"
    tattletales,
    big pills to take,
    sleet, and smog,
    and stomachache.
Since these all drive me
to distraction,
for them I'd always
use subtraction.

166

Use with Grade 2, Chapter 8, Lesson 1

 Read-Aloud Selections
Grade 2, Tape 2
Side 1, Selection 2

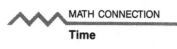 MATH CONNECTION
Time

Clocks and More Clocks

BY PAT HUTCHINS

The illustrations in this book picture the Clockmaker holding out a large pocket watch for Mr. Higgins to see as he checks the time on each clock. You will need to explain this to your children as you read the word "Look" when spoken by the Clockmaker. If an instructional clock is available, you may wish to read the story a second time, moving the hands of the clock to show the progression of time.

One day Mr. Higgins found a clock in the attic. It looked very splendid standing there. "How do I know if it's correct?" he thought.

So he went out and bought another which he placed in the bedroom.

"Three o'clock," said Mr. Higgins. "I'll see if the other clock is right."

He ran up to the attic, but the clock said one minute past three. "How do I know which one is right?" he thought.

So he went out and bought another which he placed in the kitchen. "Ten minutes to four, I'll check the others."

He ran up to the attic. The attic clock said eight minutes to four. He ran down to the bedroom. The bedroom clock said seven minutes to four.

"I still don't know which one is right," he thought.

So he went out and bought another which he placed in the hall.

"Twenty minutes past four," he said, and ran up to the attic. The attic clock said twenty-three minutes past four.

He ran down to the kitchen. The kitchen clock said twenty-five minutes past four.

He ran up to the bedroom. The bedroom clock said twenty-six minutes past four.

"This is no good at all," thought Mr. Higgins.

And he went to the Clockmaker.

5:00

"My hall clock says twenty minutes past four, my attic clock says twenty-three minutes past four, my kitchen clock says twenty-five minutes past four, my bedroom clock says twenty-six minutes past four, and I don't know which one is right!" said Mr. Higgins.

So the Clockmaker went to the house to look at the clocks.

The hall clock said five o'clock. "There's nothing wrong with this clock," said the Clockmaker. "Look!"

The kitchen clock said one minute past five.

"There!" shouted Mr. Higgins. "Your watch said five o'clock."

"But it is one minute past now!" said the Clockmaker. "Look!"

The bedroom clock said two minutes past five. "Absolutely correct!" said the Clockmaker. "Look!"

The attic clock said three minutes past five. "There's nothing wrong with this clock either," said the Clockmaker. "Look!"

"What a wonderful watch!" said Mr. Higgins.

And he went out and bought one. And since he bought his watch all his clocks have been right.

5 :01

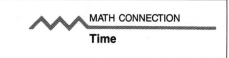
New Bicycle

BY YOLANDA NAVE

Reading this fun poem to children in your class will give them more practice with the days of the week.

Sunday I got a brand-new bike;
Monday I learned how to ride;
Tuesday I went by my grandmother's house,
And to the countryside.
Wednesday I pedaled up a hill;
Thursday I reached the top;
I'll be home Friday or Saturday—
Or as soon as I learn how to stop.

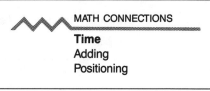
Maxie

BY MILDRED KANTROWITZ

You could set your watch by Maxie, an elderly woman who lives alone on the top floor of a brownstone—and Maxie's neighbors do! Until she deviates from her schedule one day, Maxie doesn't realize how many people rely on her.

Maxie lived in three small rooms on the top floor of an old brownstone house on Orange Street. She had lived there for many years, and every day was the same for Maxie.

Every morning, seven days a week, every morning at exactly seven o'clock, Maxie raised the shades on her three front windows.

Every morning at exactly 7:10, Maxie's large, orange cat jumped up onto the middle windowsill and sprawled there in the morning sun.

At 7:20, if you were watching Maxie's back window, you could see her raise the shade to the very top. Then she uncovered a bird cage. On the perch inside the cage was a yellow canary. He was waiting for his water dish to be filled, and it always was, if you were still watching, at 7:22.

At 8:15 every morning, Maxie's door opened with a tired squeak. Maxie's old, leather slippers made slapping sounds as she walked down the four flights of uncarpeted stairs to the front door. Outside the front door were the bottles of milk in a container. Maxie always tried to hold the door open with her left foot while she reached out to get her milk. But every morning it was just a little too far for her to reach. The door always banged shut and locked behind her.

So, at 8:20 every morning, Maxie rang the bell marked "Superintendent." The superintendent, whose name was Arthur, would open the door for Maxie and let her in with her milk.

Only Maxie and the man at the grocery store knew what she ate for breakfast, but everyone knew she drank tea. At 8:45 every morning, they could hear the whistling of her tea kettle. How Maxie loved that whistle! She loved it so much that she let it sing out for one full minute. Dogs howled, cats whined and babies bawled, but everyone knew that when the whistle stopped, it would be 8:46. And it always was.

The mailman knew more about Maxie than anyone else did. He knew that she had a sister in Chicago who sent her a Christmas card every year. He also knew when Maxie planted the flowers in her window boxes because every spring he delivered her seed catalog. Then a few weeks later he delivered packets of seeds.

Every morning at nine o'clock, Maxie walked down the stairs for the second time in her leather slippers. She went outside and put her small bag of garbage in the pail on the front stoop. Then she came back in and waited for the mailman. She walked slowly past him in the hall, watching him put mail in the slots for the other people who lived in the house.

Then she climbed the four flights of stairs again, resting at each landing. When she got to the top, Maxie went into her apartment, and the door closed after her with the same tired squeak.

One afternoon at 1:05, just as she did every afternoon at 1:05, Maxie moved the bird cage with the yellow bird in it to the front windows. It was shady and cool there now. The large, orange cat moved to the back window and sprawled there, soaking up the sun that matched the color of his fur.

"You're perfectly happy just lying there, day after day," Maxie said to the cat. "All you ever want to do is move from one windowsill to the other and watch the world go by. You don't need anyone, and no one really needs you. But you don't seem to care." Maxie turned away from the window. "I care," she said sadly. "I'm not a cat. But I might as well be." Maxie felt very tired, and she went to bed. That was Monday.

On Tuesday morning at seven o'clock, the three shades on Maxie's front windows and the one on her back window remained down. At 7:10, the large, orange cat was still asleep at the foot of Maxie's bed. And at 7:30, there were no sweet warbling sounds. That morning no one heard the sounds of Maxie's leather slippers on the stairs. Her tea kettle was filled with empty silence.

At nine o'clock, the mailman came with the daily mail. He had a seed catalog for Maxie and he waited for her to come down the stairs. Since she didn't come and this was most unusual, he decided to deliver the catalog to her door. He climbed the four flights of stairs. He knocked and waited. There was no sign of Maxie.

At 9:03, Mr. Turkle who lived on the third floor came hurrying up the stairs. At 9:05, Mr. and Mrs. Moorehouse got there from across the street. At 9:07, Mrs. Trueheart came over from next door. Susie Smith came up at 9:10 with her twin brothers. Five members of the family on the second floor made it up by 9:13. Then came Arthur, the superintendent. By 9:17, there were seventeen people, three dogs and two cats, all waiting for Maxie to open the door.

And when she didn't they all went in. They found Maxie in bed. More people came up the stairs and someone called a doctor. By the time he got there, there were forty-two grown-ups and eleven children in Maxie's small living room.

When the doctor came out of Maxie's bedroom he shook his head sadly. "Maxie isn't really sick," he said. "She's lonely. She doesn't feel loved. She doesn't feel that anyone needs her."

No one said anything for a minute. Then suddenly Mrs. Trueheart got up and walked right past the doctor and into the bedroom. "Maxie!" she shouted angrily, "you let me down. You and that warbling bird let me down! Every morning I wake up and I hear that bird. Then it's my job to wake my husband. He has the morning shift at the corner diner and he's still asleep. Why, there must be at least seventy-five people at that diner right now, waiting for their breakfasts. They'll all have to go to work on empty stomachs—all because of you and that yellow bird!"

Everyone else crowded into the bedroom. Maxie sat up in bed and listened to what they had to say. "I couldn't go to school this morning," Susie Smith said. "I missed the bus because I didn't hear your tea kettle whistle."

"The school bus never came this morning," said Mr. Turkle who drove the bus. "I didn't wake up in time. I never heard Sarah Sharpe's footsteps on my ceiling."

Sarah Sharpe was a nurse who lived just above Mr. Turkle. There were a lot of people waiting for her right now at the hospital. She always got up when she heard Maxie's door squeak.

Mr. and Mrs. Moorehouse both had very important jobs but they had missed their train that morning. Their alarm clock was Maxie's window shade.

Arthur said he hadn't swept the front steps that morning. He overslept because Maxie didn't ring his bell. He hoped no one would complain.

They all talked about it and decided that there must be about four hundred people who needed Maxie—or who needed someone else who needed Maxie— every morning.

Maxie smiled. She got out of bed and made a pot of tea. In fact, she made five pots of tea.

Each time the kettle whistled, dogs howled, cats whined and babies bawled. Maxie listened and thought about how many people were being touched by these sounds—her sounds. By 9:45 that morning, Maxie had served tea to everybody, and she was so pleased.

Use with Grade 2, Chapter 8, Lesson 5

Math Songs
Side 2, Selection 11

MATH CONNECTION
Time

CULTURAL CONNECTION
Trinidadian Folk Song

All Who Born in January

This folk song from Trinidad can serve as a starting point for studying the months of the year.

Folk Song from Trinidad

All who born in Jan-u-ar-y skip a - round.

All who born in Jan-u-ar-y skip a - round.

Tra la la la la la la   Tra la la la la la la

All who born in Jan-u-ar-y skip a - round.

Use with Grade 2, Chapter 9, Lesson 1

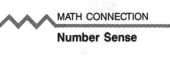

MATH CONNECTION
Number Sense

Read-Aloud Selections
Grade 2, Tape 2
Side 1, Selection 3

Two Hundred Rabbits

BY LONZO ANDERSON AND ADRIENNE ADAMS

The narrator of this story is a rabbit. This does not become readily apparent until near the end of the story, when an illustration in the book shows the rabbit scampering out from under the king's throne. You may need to stop reading at this point to explain this fact to your children, or you may wish to have them use the context clues to discover it for themselves.

*I*n my travels I came to the land of Jamais and stopped on a hill to look at the valley below.

A forest was in the middle of the view, and on one side of it stood the king's castle, surrounded by a moat full of water.

On the other side of the forest was a cottage made of stone and wood, with straw for a roof.

Someone was working in the garden near the cottage.

I love vegetables, especially lettuce, so I went down for a closer look.

The someone was a young boy. He whistled and sang as he worked.

His garden was the neatest and prettiest I had ever seen.

"Hmm," I said to myself. "This boy is really special. Great things are going to happen to him."

I decided to stop here in my travels for a while. It would be fun, as long as I could keep out of sight and just watch.

The garden had a good fence around it, so I stayed outside; but when the boy cleaned out his lettuce bed he threw over enough lettuce to fill me up, and after dark I ate it.

Early the next morning the boy set out through the forest toward the king's castle, carrying his lunch. I hustled along, keeping near him without his noticing me.

When he came out of the forest it was hard for me to follow him without being seen; but if he had looked around at me, I could have pretended to be on my way somewhere else.

The boy came to the castle moat. The guard stopped him at the drawbridge.

"What do you want?" he demanded.

"Isn't this the Festival Day at the castle?"

"It is," the guard replied, stiff as his staff.

"I wish to entertain the king," the boy said, "and maybe he will give me a steady job."

"Oh?" The guard raised an eyebrow. "And what can you do to entertain the king?"

"I can stand on my head longer than almost anybody."

"The king would not be amused," the guard said.

"I can skate faster than . . ."

"In *summer*?" The guard raised his other eyebrow.

"I can swim . . ."

The guard was shaking his head.

"Then what *do* people do to entertain the king?" the boy asked.

"Some sing," the guard said.

The boy went into the forest to practice singing. He sang, and the birds all flew out of the forest in horror. Even I felt like stopping up my ears.

"Oh, this will never do!" I said to myself. "If only he could think of something better!"

The boy went again to the guard and asked, "What else do people do to entertain the king?"

"Some play musical instruments," the guard said.

The boy ran home for his fiddle and went into the forest to practice playing. The squirrels and chipmunks and foxes and wolves all came to scold him, but I kept as quiet as I could. I was still panting from running to keep up with him.

"Oh, this is not good," I said to myself. I could hear the sounds of the festival at the castle. "If only he could think of a fine idea before it is too late!"

The boy took his fiddle home, then scampered once more to the guard.

"What else do people do?" he asked, out of breath.

"Some juggle," the guard said.

The festival was almost half over. The boy did not stop to listen to the happy roar in the courtyard. He hurried into the forest to practice juggling.

He juggled with sticks and stones and old pine cones, but they all slipped through his hands or fell on his head. The birds and animals watched him and sneered and jeered.

He sat down on a log. My heart ached for him, he looked so discouraged. Soon the festival would be over, and he would have lost his chance to entertain the king.

Suddenly, an old woman was standing there.

The boy jumped up and bowed.

"You look sad," the old woman said.

He smiled. "I didn't mean to," he said. "Won't you sit down and rest?"

"Thank you, I think I will," the old woman said.

They sat together on the log.

"You do have troubles, though," she said.

He sighed. "Life is more difficult than I ever thought, when it comes to making my way in the world."

"Tell me about it," she said.

As he told her, he shared his sausages with her. He gave her more than half. I could see his eyes as he looked at her thin, old face; he thought she was starving.

"But," she said when he had finished his story, "the best way to catch the king's attention is to show him something that no one else has in all the world."

"Yes," the boy said, "but what?"

"Do you know how to make a slippery-elm slide whistle?" the old woman asked.

"Why, yes," he said. "Doesn't everyone?"

"Let me see you do it," she said.

He found a slippery-elm tree. It had many twigs of the right size and smoothness for a whistle, but one in particular wriggled, as if to catch his eye, while all the others kept still.

He cut the enchanted twig with his sheath knife and made it the right length.

The old woman was watching him like a hawk. She nodded approvingly as he cut and notched and sliced and tapped until it was finished.

"What a clever boy!" I said to myself. Never had I seen a whistle like this.

"Blow it," the old woman said.

He blew, and by sliding the lower part of the twig up and down inside the slippery bark as he blew into the mouthpiece, he was able to play a tune.

At the sound all the rabbits that lived in the forest came running, and crowded about him.

"A magic whistle!" the boy cried, and I danced for joy.

"Blow it again," the old woman said.

He blew, and the rabbits lined up like soldiers.

There were twenty rows of them, ten in each row but the last. In the last row there were only nine.

"Tch-tch!" the old woman said. "How annoying. A hundred and ninety-nine rabbits. They don't come out even. I'm sorry."

"But what does it matter? This is wonderful!"

The boy looked at the rabbits, and they looked at him as if they were ready to follow him anywhere.

"Atten-*tion!*" he cried.

The rabbits stood straight up, like soldiers.

"Forward, *march!*"

The rabbits marched through the forest toward the king's castle, the boy leading them with short steps so as not to leave them behind. He played a bouncy little tune on his whistle, nodding and bowing his thanks to the old woman.

I was so excited I was shivering. What a wonderful thing it was, that rabbit parade! But oh, was it too late for the festival? How I hoped the boy would be in time!

Out of the forest the rabbits went marching. They were having such fun I was tempted to march with them. But I was a stranger there, and the old woman's magic was not for me.

The festival was not over yet. Some people were coming out of the courtyard, but others were going in.

The king looked out of his window and saw the marvelous marching rabbits. He called to invite them to cross the drawbridge, and they did. And so did I, losing myself in the crowd.

The king came down from his room and sat on his courtyard throne to review the parade.

In the excitement I crawled under the throne from behind, to keep out of the way and have a good view.

"Halt!" the king shouted suddenly.

The boy stopped the parade and the marching tune.

"That last row!" the king said crossly. "It doesn't come out even!"

"True, Your Majesty," the boy said, bowing.

"Well, it looks silly," the king complained. "It looks ragged. *Away with those last nine rabbits!*"

"But, Your Majesty," the boy said, "that would break their hearts!"

"Hmph," the king said. "I suppose it would. Hmmm . . . *Then get another rabbit!*"

"But Your Majesty," the boy said, "there is not one other rabbit in our whole forest."

"Oh," His Majesty said, scowling. He cocked his head and thought, while I held my breath, waiting.

Then, "*Away with all of you!*" he roared.

Now I had no choice. How could I just sit there and not help?

I popped out from under the king's throne and took my place in the last row of rabbits.

That made everything all right.

The boy smiled. He took up his tune where he had left off, and gave the signal to march. We paraded in front of the king, who clapped his hands and cried:

"This will make my court the most popular court in the whole world!"

Oh, well. I was tired of traveling anyway.

The Snow Parade

BY BARBARA BRENNER

Everyone loves a parade. Andrew Barclay starts a snow parade of one. Soon, so many people join that there are too many to count!

"**W**ho wants to make a snow parade?" asked Andrew Barclay.

"I can't," said his sister.

"I won't," said his brother.

"Then I'll make a parade by myself," said Andrew.

So Andrew Barclay went off alone to make a parade in the snow.

He marched along in his new red boots.

Marched and marched.

All by himself.

And he was the only *one* in that parade.

Pretty soon he met a spotted dog.

"What are you doing," the dog asked him.

Andrew answered, "I'm making a parade."

"*One* isn't enough for a parade," said the dog.

"Then you march with me," said Andrew.

"I can't march," said the dog, "but I'll run."

So Andrew marched and the dog ran.

Now there were *two* of them making a parade.

After a while a duck swam over.

"What are you doing?" asked the duck.

"We're making a parade," said Andrew.

"*Two* is too few for a parade," said the duck.

"I'll swim along with the *two* of you."

So, Andrew marched, the dog ran, and the duck swam.

Now there were *three* of them parading.

A rabbit came by.

"What's this?" asked the rabbit.

Andrew said, "This is a parade."

"I don't call *three* a parade," said the rabbit.

"Then why don't you come along?"

"I will," said the rabbit. I'll hop along in the back."

So Andrew marched, the dog ran, the duck swam, and the rabbit hopped along in the back.

Now there were *four* of them making a parade.

A pigeon flew by. "What's going on down there?" called the pigeon.

"A parade," Andrew called back.

The pigeon said, "It takes more than *four* to make a parade."

"Then you come, too," said Andrew.

"Good idea," said the pigeon.

"I'll fly along on the side."

Pigeon flew.

Rabbit hopped.

Duck waddled.

Dog ran.

Andrew marched.

Now there were *five* in the parade.

A policeman rode by on his horse. "What are you doing?" he asked.

Andrew said, "We're making a parade."

"Oh, no," said the policeman. "*Five* is a handful but it's not a parade. We'll have to come along with you."

The policeman rode at the front.

He made *six*.

And his horse made *seven*.

Now there were seven in the snow parade.

An old man with a beard joined.

He made *eight*.

A boy pulling a sled joined.

Nine.

And the girl on the sled made *ten*.

Now there were *ten* in the parade.

When the policeman blew his whistle, they began to sing a parade song.

Andrew sang the words.

The dog barked.

The duck quacked.

The pigeon cooed.

The rabbit chittered.

The horse neighed.

And the old man waved his cane in time to the music, while the boy and girl on the sled sang harmony.

Now others joined the parade.

Mothers with baby carriages.

Boys and girls on bicycles.

Folks in buggies.

People came out of their houses and even the squirrels came out of their holes in the trees to join the parade.

Ten. Twenty. Thirty. Forty. Fifty. One Hundred. Five Hundred. More.

Soon there were so many you just couldn't count them all.

And Andrew Barclay said, "Now this is what I call a parade."

Use with Grade 2, Chapter 10, Lesson 1

Read-Aloud Selections
Grade 2, Tape 2
Side 2, Selection 1

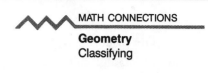

MATH CONNECTIONS

Geometry
Classifying

Surprises

BY JEAN CONDER SOULE
FROM *THE RANDOM HOUSE BOOK OF POETRY FOR CHILDREN*

*Suprises come in all shapes and size. Let children draw a surprise they would like to give
someone. Then have them draw a picture of the kind of container that would put the
surprise in so no one would guess what it was.*

Surprises are round
Or long or tallish.
Surprises are square
Or flat or smallish.

Surprises are wrapped
With paper and bow,
And hidden in closets
Where secrets won't show.

Surprises are often
Good things to eat;
A get-well toy or
A birthday treat.

Surprises come
In such interesting sizes—
I LIKE
SURPRISES!

MATH CONNECTION
Geometry
Classifying

CULTURAL CONNECTION
African Story

The Village of Round and Square Houses

BY ANN GRIFALCONI

The eruption of a volcano causes the people of a village to look at one another differently. Tos, the village of round and square houses, really does exist in the Cameroons of Central Africa.

It was not until I was almost full-grown and left my village
That I found our village was like no other.
For the men live in SQUARE houses, and the women, in ROUND ones!
To me, this seemed the natural order of things. . . .
"But what is it like," you ask.
I will tell you how it was—and is—for me.

I grew up on my grandmother's farm in the village of Tos
That lies at the foot of Naka Mountain in the Bameni Hills of west Africa.
We planted yams and corn and tobacco
And the finest coffee grown in the Cameroons.
Our village was always happy and peaceful—
A good place for any boy or girl to grow up.

Every evening, after a day of work in the fields—
Uncle Domo and Gran'pa Oma came to our round house for supper.
We children would hurry to put out the low, wooden stool for Gran'pa Oma
(For he was the eldest, and closer to the ancestor spirits).
Then we would unroll the grass mat for Uncle Domo, the next oldest,
As was only proper and respectful.

And there they would sit proudly in their bright robes—
Gran'pa Olma above, seated on his stool, hands on knees—
And Uncle Domo seated below.
Then they would ask to see the children!
One by one we would come forward from the narrow doorway. . .
And one by one, we would be lifted to sit upon those high and bony knees,
And Gran'pa would ask each one of us, "What have you learned today?"

We would squirm and make an answer
And wriggle off those sharp knees
And run to help Mama and Gran'ma Tika prepare the meal to come.
Supper might be fish or rabbit or ground-nut stew or yams—

But always *I* would be the one to pound and soften the white cassava root,
To make the *fou-fou* we eat at every meal.
Then Mama would cook the *fou-fou* and beat it 'til it was white and fluffy
And she would pile the food into big bowls with round handles—
Just right for our small hands to hold.

Then we would march into the big round room—
Our bare feet gripping the earthen floor.
The little ones went first, carrying the bowl of heated water and towels
To wash the hands before and after eating.
Then the older ones would carry in the stew,
Spicy and steaming—smelling oh, so good!
And I would come in last bearing the *fou-fou!*

Gran'pa, as the eldest, would always eat first,
Dipping the first three fingers of one hand into the *fou-fou*—
Scooping up a small portion which he dipped *quickly* into the stew bowl,
To flavor each bite with the spicy meat and juices!
Then, in order of age—Gran'ma, Uncle Domo, and sometimes Mama
(If she left the cook fire) would finish their meal in the same way,
And we children would follow last—making sure to leave the bowl clean!

After supper, when the men went back to their square house
To smoke, and talk of farming and fishing and the old days of the hunt,
Gran'pa would leave some tobacco for Gran'ma.
(He knew she liked to smoke it later—when everything was peaceful.)

Then she would sit alone in the moonlight, looking up at the dark slope
Of Naka Mountain, rising high above. . . .

I remember one night I sat beside her—Gran'ma Tika took a last puff on her pipe
Then pointed with it to the sky above our village.
"You see old Mother Naka smoking so peacefully there?"
I leaned way back and looked up to see old Naka's breath
Rising in lazy puffs of smoke, soft and gray in the night sky.

"And you remember that sometimes in the night
We hear old Naka snoring in her sleep?"
I nodded, pleased that Gran'ma felt I was old enough to notice such things.
"Well, it is by these signs that we know she is content.
Now, we live in peace with Naka and the spirits of our ancestors,
But it was not always so!"

Gran'ma fixed me with a stare
And began to rock with a tale. . .
For she was the best storyteller in the whole village!

"In the days of long, long ago,
The people of this village lived
In houses of any sort, either square or round,
It did not matter.

"Then, one peaceful night
Before anyone alive remembers
Old Naka began to groan and rumble
And awoke from a long sleep!

"The villagers were frightened
And ran out of their houses
And hid in the bushes
At the foot of the mountain.

"A great wind came up
And the ancestor spirits in the trees
Cried out to warn them—
Even the rocks began to tremble!

"Suddenly, the black night
Was split open like a coconut!
And a great white burst of light
Rose like the sun!

"Then the voice of our mother Naka
Thundered out over all:
BOOM! BA-BOOM! BA-BOOM!

"And the people cried out to Naka,
And prayed where they were lying down,
Hands pressing the earth, asking:
'What have we done to so anger you?'

"All through the night
Old Naka spoke to them
Shouting her anger to the skies
As red rivers of lava flowed down her sides.

"The morning sun rose
But no one could see him—
The anger of Naka was too great
And ashes and smoke filled the air.

"Finally—
No one remembers when—
Naka spoke no more. . . .

"Slowly—carefully—
The people lifted their heads and looked about:
Everything was covered with ashes—
Even themselves!

"Everyone looked like a gray ghost—
No one knew who stood next to them
Or who came behind. . . .

"So they stood there—
Trembling with fear—
But grateful to be alive:
NAKA HAD SPARED THEM!

"Still covered with ashes—
The men, women, and children
Faced the mountain together
And went back to claim their homes.

"But when they came to the burned-out village,
Only two houses were left standing:
One SQUARE—   And one ROUND!

"The people saw that only
These two houses had been spared by Naka
And they wondered to themselves:
Why these? Was it a sign?'

"But the village chief had no time
For such questions—
And he called them together:
'We must begin to rebuild our village now!'

"He pointed to the ash-covered people:
'You! TALL GRAY THINGS!
You go live in the SQUARE house!'

"'And you! ROUND GRAY THINGS—
Go live in the round house!'

"'And you! SMALL GRAY THINGS over there!
You go pick the small gray stones out of the fields
So we can plant our crops again!'

"And so it was done.
The women lived in the round house with the children
And the women talked and laughed—
Preparing food for everyone.

"The men stayed in the square house
And told each other tall stories
And planted yams and corn
Each day, in the new, rich soil.

"And the children made a game
Out of clearing the fields of small, gray stones
And went swimming and fishing in the long afternoons...

"And no one forgot to thank Naka
For sparing their lives
And giving them back such fine crops
From her good earth."

Gran'ma smiled down at me: "And so you see it has been to this day!
For the women have decided they *enjoy* getting together
To talk and to laugh and to sing
And the men have become *used* to being together,
And relaxing in their own place.

"And the children? Osa—is it not true?
The children still keep the fields clear of little gray stones?"
"Yes!" I laughed. "And we still swim and play in the afternoon—
But we bring home the fish we catch for supper,
And we all get together then!"

Gran'ma laughed too: "So you see, Osa, we live together peacefully here—
Because each one has a place to be apart, and a time to be together...."
She took me by the hand and turned back to the round house.
"And that is how our way came about and will continue—

"'Til Naka speaks again!"

Use with Grade 2, Chapter 11, Lesson 1

 Read-Aloud Selections
Grade 2, Tape 2
Side 2, Selection 2

MATH CONNECTION
Fractions

How Many Ways Can You Cut a Pie?

BY JANE BELK MONCURE

An understanding of parts of this story is dependent on the illustrations in the book. Descriptions of these illustrations are given in parentheses. To help your children visualize the pie divisions given at the end of this story, draw pies on the chalkboard and divide them as shown.

The Library—A Magic Castle

*Come to the magic castle
When you are growing tall.
Rows upon rows of Word Windows
Line every single wall.
They reach up high,
As high as the sky,
And you want to open them all.
For every time you open one,
A new adventure has begun.*

Dan opened a Word Window. He read. . .(Illustration shows Dan reading a book.)

One fall day Squirrel saw this sign. (Illustration shows a sign reading: Pie Contest Today. Signed, Pig)

"I will bake my best acorn pie for the pie contest," she said.

And she did.

The pie was still hot when Mouse came by.

"My," said Mouse. "What a fine pie. Will you cut the pie in two pieces...one half for me, one half for you?"

"No," said Squirrel. "This pie is for the pie contest. If I win, I will share my pie with you."

Then Frog came by. "My," said Frog. "What a fine pie. I do like acorn pie," he said. "Will you cut the pie in three pieces...one piece for you...one for mouse... and one for me?"

"No," said Squirrel. "This pie is for the pie contest. If I win, I will share my pie with you."

The pie was still hot, so Squirrel put it in the window to cool. Then the three friends went for a walk in the woods.

While they were gone, Pig came by.

"My," said Pig. "What a fine pie. I will try just one little bite of pie. Very good," she said.

Then Pig ate another bite. "It is just right," she said.

Pig ate and ate and ate until she cleaned the plate.

Just then Squirrel and her friends came by.

"My pie!" cried Squirrel. "Why did you eat my pie?"

"Was your pie for my pie contest today?" asked Pig.

"It was," said Squirrel.

Pig took something out of her pocket.

"Surprise! You win my pie contest," she said. "Your pie was the very best."

"That is not fair," said Mouse.

"Not fair at all," said Frog. "You ate the whole pie that we were going to share."

"I did not mean to eat the whole pie," said Pig. "I will try to make things right."

Pig ran outside and found more acorns.

"Squirrel makes the best pies of all," said Pig. "Maybe she will make one more."

Squirrel did make one more pie. She cut it into four pieces, so everyone had a fair share.

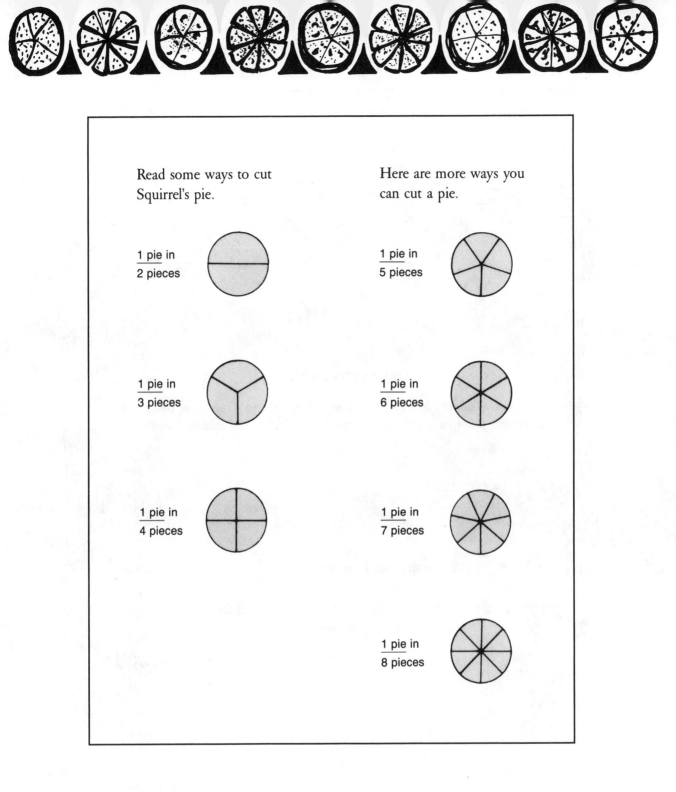

Read some ways to cut
Squirrel's pie.

Here are more ways you
can cut a pie.

1 pie in
2 pieces

1 pie in
5 pieces

1 pie in
3 pieces

1 pie in
6 pieces

1 pie in
4 pieces

1 pie in
7 pieces

1 pie in
8 pieces

A Sum

BY LEWIS CARROLL

Lewis Carroll sums up fractions in this poem. Given the choice of two halves, three thirds, or quarters four (you need to explain this phrase), which would children choose?

I give thee all, I can no more,
　　Though small thy share may be:
Two halves, three thirds, and quarters four
　　Is all I bring to thee.

Use with Grade 2, Chapter 12, Lesson 1

 Read-Aloud Selections
Grade 2, Tape 2
Side 2, Selection 3

MATH CONNECTIONS

Multiplying
Dividing
Adding
Subtracting
Counting

The Doorbell Rang

BY PAT HUTCHINS

Children can work backward to find out how many cookies Ma made—and they can use their imaginations to find out how many cookies Grandma made!

"I've made some cookies for tea," said Ma.

"Good," said Victoria and Sam. "We're starving."

"Share them between yourselves," said Ma. "I made plenty."

"That's six each," said Sam and Victoria.

"They look as good as Grandma's," said Victoria.

"They smell as good as Grandma's," said Sam.

"No one makes cookies like Grandma," said Ma as the doorbell rang.

It was Tom and Hannah from next door.

"Come in," said Ma. "You can share the cookies."

"That's three each," said Sam and Victoria.

"They smell good as your Grandma's," said Tom.

"And look as good," said Hannah.

"No one makes cookies like Grandma," said Ma as the doorbell rang.

It was Peter and his little brother.

"Come in," said Ma. "You can share the cookies."

"That's two each," said Victoria and Sam.

"They look as good as your Grandma's," said Peter. "And smell as good."

"Nobody makes cookies like Grandma," said Ma as the doorbell rang.

It was Joy and Simon with their four cousins.

"Come in," said Ma. "You can share the cookies."

"That's one each," said Sam and Victoria.

"They smell as good as your Grandma's," said Joy.

"And look as good," said Simon.

"No one makes cookies like Grandma," said Ma as the doorbell rang and rang.

"Oh dear," said Ma as the children stared at the cookies on their plates. "Perhaps you'd better eat them before we open the door."

"We'll wait," said Sam.

It was Grandma with an enormous tray of cookies.

"How nice to have so many friends to share them with," said Grandma. "It's a good thing I made a lot!"

"And no one makes cookies like Grandma," said Ma as the doorbell rang.

Use with Grade 2, Chapter 12, Lesson 3

MATH CONNECTIONS

Multiplying
Dividing
Adding
Subtracting

Ten Little Squirrels

TRADITIONAL

To build children's comprehension of multiplication and division, have them act out or draw the groups of squirrels. You may want to discuss the man having a gun with the children, or you may want to revise the poem.

Ten little squirrels sat on a tree,
The first two said, "Why, what do we see?"
The next two said, "A man with a gun,"
The next two said, "Let's run, let's run,"
The next two said, "Let's hide in the shade,"
The next two said, "Why, we're not afraid!"
But, "Bang!" went the gun, and away they
    all run.

Use with Grade 2, Chapter 12, Lesson 3

Math Songs
Side 2, Selection 12

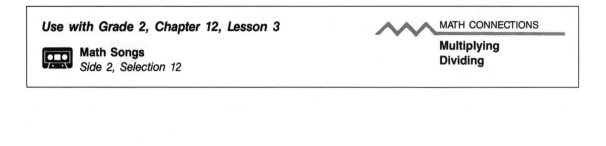

MATH CONNECTIONS
Multiplying
Dividing

Hop Up, My Ladies

When discussing this song, you will need to tell children how many ladies there are. You also may have to explain that when a horse carries double, it carries two people.

1. Did you ev - er go to meet - ing, Un - cle Joe, Un - cle Joe?
2. Will your horse__ car - ry dou - ble, Un - cle Joe, Un - cle Joe?

Did you ev - er go to meet - ing, Un - cle Joe?____
Will your horse__ car - ry dou - ble, Un - cle Joe?____

Did you ev - er go to meet - ing, Un - cle Joe, Un - cle Joe?
Will your horse__ car - ry dou - ble, Un - cle Joe, Un - cle Joe?

D.C. al Fine

Don't mind the weath - er so the wind don't blow.
Don't mind the weath - er so the wind don't blow.

197

Use with Grade 2, Chapter 13, Lesson 1

Read-Aloud Selections
Grade 2, Tape 2
Side 2, Selection 4

MATH CONNECTIONS

Adding
Subtracting
Money

Too Many Books!

BY CAROLINE FELLER BAUER

Maralou loves to read. Soon, she has so many books she doesn't know what to do!

Maralou loved books, even as a baby. When Maralou learned to read, she read all of the time.

She read at the breakfast table.

She read on the bus to school.

She read in the bathtub.

She read while she jumped rope

. . .or tried to.

Every week, Maralou took her wagon to the library to borrow books. The following week, Maralou brought the books back and borrowed more.

One day during Book Week, Maralou's Aunt Molly *gave* her a book. Fantastic! Now that she owned her own book, she could read it over and over again.

Maralou wanted more books. She asked for books whenever someone wanted to give her a present.

She was given books for her birthday,

For Halloween,

. . .and even for the Fourth of July.

Maralou also earned money so she could buy books.

She cat sat.

She sold lemonade.

She had a garage sale.

She tried to sell her little brother

. . .but that didn't work.

After a while, Maralou had a lot of books. Mom and Dad built shelves for the books but there still wasn't enough room.

There were books in the bathtub,

on every table,

all over the floor,

. . .and even in the refrigerator.

Maralou had too many books! Mom couldn't get out the front door. Dad couldn't get in the back door. But Maralou still loved books and wanted more to read.

How could she make room?

Then Maralou had an idea. Maybe other people would love books too! So she decided to give some books away.

She gave a book to a little boy on his way to school.

She gave a book to the mail carrier.

She left books at the doctor's office

                        . . .and at the playground.

Soon the whole town was reading all the time. People bought books, borrowed books, and traded books. The town was bulging with books.

The mayor called the librarian in the next town to see if they would like to have some books. They did, and it wasn't long before *all* the nearby towns were borrowing and trading and reading and sharing books.

But Maralou didn't notice.

She sat in front of the library

                 . . .reading a book.

Bit by Bit

BY LISA YOUNT

Rosa Hernández would like to own a computer. With the help of her family and neighbors, she earns enough money to buy a computer of her own. The story also illustrates what a savings account is and how interest is accumulated.

"I would like to get a computer," said Rosa Hernández one morning.

Ramón, Rosa's brother, laughed at her. "What do you know about computers?" he said.

"I've used a computer in school," Rosa told him. "I know they can do many things. They can make lists and they can add numbers."

"We can't buy you a computer," said Rosa's father. "They cost a lot of money."

"Some don't," said Rosa. She showed her father an advertisement in one of the newspapers.

"That's still more than we can give you," Rosa's mother said.

"I know. I'll try and earn the money myself," Rosa said. "This summer I'll work for people in the neighborhood. I'll save the money I earn and buy a computer. My teacher says computers break everything we tell them into little parts called bits. That's how I'll get money for my computer—bit by bit."

"I'll help you," said Ramón. "I can give you some of the money I earn from my paper route."

"We can help, too," said Rosa's mother and father. "We will match the amount of money you earn each week. If you make five dollars, we will give you five dollars. Then you will have ten dollars."

"I'll get started right now!" said Rosa.

The next day Rosa and Ramón went to the park. "Sometimes people leave bottles here," Ramón said. "The market will give us money for bringing them back. I'll show you which kind. We can get a dime for the little bottles and two dimes for the big bottles."

Ramón and Rosa picked up three little bottles and one big one. They put them in Rosa's wagon.

On their way home, Ramón and Rosa met their neighbor Mrs. Yee.

"That's a big wagon," Mrs. Yee said. "It looks like it holds a lot."

"Yes," Rosa said. "We use it to carry bottles. We are going to get money for them. We are saving to buy a computer."

"I'll give you money, too, if you will help me," said Mrs. Yee. "It's hard for me to carry all my things from the market. If you bring your wagon and carry the things I buy home, I'll give you two dollars every week."

"Thank you, Mrs. Yee," cried Rosa.

A week later, Rosa went to the bank. She had two dollars from Mrs. Yee. She had $1.10 from bottles she had picked up that week. She had earned $3.10, so she got $3.10 from her mother and father. Ramónhad given her $3.00 from his paper route.

"I would like to put my money in the bank," Rosa told the woman at the bank.

The woman gave Rosa a savings book. It showed how much money she put in the bank.

"If you leave your money here for a while, you will earn more money," the woman told her. "We give you money while the bank makes use of your money. That kind of money is called interest. The interest will be only a little bit at first. But it can grow."

Rosa asked other people in her neighborhood what work she could do for them.

"Mrs. Long and I are going away for a week," Mr. Long said. "We need someone to watch our bird. We'll pay you fifty cents a day to do that."

For the rest of the summer, Rosa watched some pets for her neighbors. Each time Rosa earned money for her work, she put it in the bank. The list of numbers in her bank book got longer and longer.

At last it was the week before school. Rosa got her money out of the bank. It was a surprise for Rosa to see how much she had made, but she still didn't have quite as much as she needed.

"Let's go look at some computers, anyway." Rosa said to the family. "At least we can look at the computer I want." So off they all went.

But the computer store had a surprise for Rosa. The computer she wanted was on sale that week!

The woman counted Rosa's money. "You have more than you need for this computer," she said.

"I earned it," Rosa said smiling, "bit by bit."

INDEX

●INDEX BY TITLE●

Ai Hai Yo, 112
All of Our Noses Are Here, 58
All Who Born in January, 173
Animals' Houses, 115
Annie's Pet, 47
Ants at the Olympics, The, 89

Band-Aids, 120
Banza, The, 128
Birthday Basket for Tía, A, 140
Bit by Bit, 208
Bleezer's Ice Cream, 86

Caps for Sale, 8
Cats, 3
Cats of Kilkenny, The, 71
Chook, Chook, Chook, 76
Clocks and More Clocks, 167
Cottage, 104
Couldn't We Have a Turtle Instead?, 26
Counting Rhyme, A, 31
Counting Song, 60
Creature in the Classroom, The, 75
Crickets, The, 73

Don't Ask Me, 148
Doorbell Rang, The, 193
Draw a Bucket of Water, 24

Enormous Turnip, The, 64

Face of the Clock, The, 110
Fifteen Cents, 94
Five Brown Teddies, 70
Five Fat Turkeys, 134
Five Little Ducks, 68

Going over the Sea, 55
Graceful Elephant, The, 66

Harvest, 2
Hattie and the Fox, 21
Hello Song, 13
Hokey Pokey, 7
Homework Machine, 144
Hop Up, My Ladies, 196
Hot Cross Buns, 151
Hot Thirsty Day, A, 162
How Big Is a Foot?, 152
How Many Ways Can You Cut a Pie?, 189
Hugs and Kisses, 88
Hurry, Little Pony, 32

If You're Happy, 20

Jesse Bear, What Will You Wear?, 40
Johnny Works with One Hammer, 67

Knee-High Man, The, 98

Leopard Finds Gold, 123
List, A, 105
Little Fish, 19

Marrog, The, 121
Maxie, 170
Mexicali Soup, 80
Mitten, The, 4
Moira's Birthday, 50
Money's Funny, 43
Morris Goes to School, 100
Most Wonderful Egg in the World, The, 113
Mud for Sale, 91

New Bicycle, 169
New Coat for Anna, A, 154
Ninety-Nine Pockets, 158

Oak Tree, The, 108
Okay Everybody, 28
One, Two, Buckle My Shoe, 54
Over in the Meadow, 29

Peanut Butter, 44
Penelope Gets Wheels, 149
Poem for a Pickle, A, 93
Pop Goes the Weasel, 95

Snow Parade, The, 179
Song of the Dragon, 143
Spring in China, 157
Spring Is Coming, 97
Square as a House, 36
Story Snail, The, 135
Sum, A, 192
Surprises, 182

Tatum's Favorite Shape, 33
Ten in a Bed, 78
Ten Little Fingers, 77

Ten Little Squirrels, 195
Ten Puppies (*Diez Pierritos*), 85
There are Big Waves, 11
There Was an Old Man Who Said, 133
There Was an Old Man with a Beard, 132
There Were Two Wrens, 72
This Old Man, 63
Thousand Pails of Water, A, 145
Three Little Monkeys, 49
Too Many Books!, 198
Too Many Daves, 53
Too Many Hopkins, 116
Too Much Noise, 14
Two Greedy Bears, 37
Two Hundred Rabbits, 174
Two Loaves, 96

Using Subtraction, 166

Village of Round and Square Houses, The, 183

What is Pink?, 12
Who Has the Penny?, 46
Who Wants One?, 61
Why Coyote Isn't Blue, 118

•INDEX OF MATH CONNECTIONS•

ADDING

Annie's Pet, 47
Band-Aids, 120
Banza, The, 128
Bit by Bit, 200
Bleezer's Ice Cream, 86
Chook, Chook, Chook, 76
Clocks and More Clocks, 167
Cottage, 104
Couldn't We Have a Turtle Instead?, 26
Counting Rhyme, A, 31
Creature in the Classroom, The, 75
Crickets, The, 73
Don't Ask Me, 148
Doorbell Rang, The, 193
Enormous Turnip, The, 64
Fifteen Cents, 94
Five Fat Turkeys, 134
Graceful Elephant, The, 66
Hattie and the Fox, 21
Homework Machine, 144
Hot Thirsty Day, A, 162
Johnny Works with One Hammer, 67
Marrog, The, 121
Maxie, 170
Mitten, The, 4
Morris Goes to School, 100
Mud for Sale, 91
Ninety-Nine Pockets, 158
Pop Goes the Weasel, 95
Snow Parade, The, 179
Ten Little Fingers, 77
Ten Little Squirrels, 195
There Was an Old Man with a Beard, 132
There Was an Old Man Who Said, 133
There Were Two Wrens, 72
Thousand Pails of Water, A, 145
Three Little Monkeys, 49
Too Many Books!, 198
Too Many Hopkins, 116
Too Much Noise, 14
Why Coyote Isn't Blue, 118

CLASSIFYING

Caps for Sale, 8
Hello Song, 13
Square as a House, 36
Surprises, 182
There are Big Waves, 11
What Is Pink?, 12

COMPARING

Couldn't We Have a Turtle Instead?, 26
Knee-High Man, The, 98
Most Wonderful Egg in the World, The, 113
Okay Everybody, 28
Two Greedy Bears, 37

COUNTING

All of Our Noses Are Here, 58
Band-Aids, 120
Banza, The, 128
Bleezer's Ice Cream, 86
Counting Rhyme, A, 31
Counting Song, 60
Crickets, The, 73
Draw a Bucket of Water, 24
Five Fat Turkeys, 134
Going over the Sea, 55

Graceful Elephant, The, 66
Hattie and the Fox, 21
Hurry, Little Pony, 32
Johnny Works with One Hammer, 67
Leopard Finds Gold, 123
Mitten, The, 4
Moira's Birthday, 50
Morris Goes to School, 100
One, Two, Buckle My Shoe, 54
Over in the Meadow, 29
Snow Parade, The, 179
Ten in a Bed, 78
Ten Little Fingers, 77
Ten Puppies (*Diez Perritos*), 85
There Were Two Wrens, 72
This Old Man, 63
Thousand Pails of Water, A, 145
Too Many Daves, 53
Too Many Hopkins, 116
Too Much Noise, 14
Who Wants One?, 61

DIVIDING

Doorbell Rang, The, 193
Hop Up, My Ladies, 196
Ten Little Squirrels, 195

ESTIMATING

How Big Is a Foot?, 153
Leopard Finds Gold, 123
Marrog, The, 121
New Coat for Anna, A, 154
Song of the Dragon, 143
Spring in China, 157

FRACTIONS

How Many Ways Can You Cut a Pie?, 189
Tatum's Favorite Shape, 33
Two Greedy Bears, 37
Sum, A, 192

GEOMETRY

Animals' Houses, 115
Couldn't We Have a Turtle Instead?, 26
Most Wonderful Egg in the World, The, 113
Ninety-Nine Pockets, 158
Square as a House, 36
Surprises, 182
Tatum's Favorite Shape, 33
Two Loaves, 96
Village of Round and Square Houses, The, 183

MEASURING

Ants at the Olympics, The, 89
Couldn't We Have a Turtle Instead?, 26
How Big Is a Foot?, 152
Knee-High Man, The, 98
Marrog, The, 121
Most Wonderful Egg in the World, The, 113
New Coat for Anna, A, 158
Okay Everybody, 28
Spring in China, 157
Spring Is Coming, 97
Two Loaves, 96

MONEY

Annie's Pet, 47
Bit by Bit, 200

Caps for Sale, 8
Fifteen Cents, 94
Homework Machine, 144
Hot Cross Buns, 151
Hot Thirsty Day, A, 162
Money's Funny, 43
Morris Goes to School, 100
Mud for x Sale, 91
Penelope Gets Wheels, 149
Poem for a Pickle, A, 93
Pop Goes the Weasel, 95
Too Many Books!, 198
Who Has the Penny?, 46

Leopard Finds Gold, 123
Marrog, The, 121
Moira's Birthday, 50
Ninety-Nine Pockets, 162
One, Two, Buckle My Shoe, 54
Snow Parade, The, 179
Song of the Dragon, 143
Story Snail, The, 135
There Was an Old Man Who Said, 133
Thousand Pails of Water, A, 145
Too Many Daves, 53
Too Many Hopkins, 116
Two Hundred Rabbits, 174

MULTIPLYING

Counting Rhyme, A, 31
Don't Ask Me, 148
Doorbell Rang, The, 193
Hop Up, My Ladies, 196
Hot Thirsty Day, A, 162
Leopard Finds Gold, 123
Mud for x Sale, 91
Ten Little Squirrels, 195
Why Coyote Isn't Blue, 118

NUMBER SENSE

Ants at the Olympics, The, 89
Band-Aids, 120
Birthday Basket for Tía, A, 140
Bleezer's Ice Cream, 86
Cottage, 104
Doorbell Rang, The, 193
Going over the Sea, 55
Hugs and Kisses, 88

PATTERNING

Hello Song, 13
If You're Happy, 20
Little Fish, 19
Too Much Noise, 14

POSITIONING

Caps for Sale, 8
Cats, 3
Hokey Pokey, 7
Mitten, The, 4

SUBTRACTING

Annie's Pet, 47
Band-Aids, 120
Banza, The, 128
Bit by Bit, 200
Cats of Kilkenny, The, 71
Cottage, 104

Creature in the Classroom, The, 75

Don't Ask Me, 148

Doorbell Rang, The, 193

Five Brown Teddies, 70

Five Fat Turkeys, 134

Five Little Ducks, 68

Graceful Elephant, The, 66

Hattie and the Fox, 21

Homework Machine, 144

Hot Thirsty Day, A, 162

Marrog, The, 121

Mexicali Soup, 80

Mitten, The, 4

Morris Goes to School, 100

Pop Goes the Weasel, 95

Snow Parade, The, 179

Ten in a Bed, 78

Ten Little Fingers, 77

Ten Puppies (Diez Perritos), 85

Ten Little Squirrels, 195

There Was an Old Man with a Beard, 132

There Were Two Wrens, 72

Thousand Pails of Water, A, 145

Three Little Monkeys, 49

Too Many Books!, 198

Too Many Hopkins, 116

Too Much Noise, 14

Using Subtraction, 166

TIME

Ai Hai Yo, 112

All Who Born in January, 173

Ants at the Olympics, The, 89

Clocks and More Clocks, 167

Creature in the Classroom, The, 75

Face of the Clock, The, 110

Fifteen Cents, 94

Harvest, 2

Hugs and Kisses, 88

Jesse Bear, What Will Wear?, 40

List, A, 105

Maxie, 170

Moira's Birthday, 50

Morris Goes to School, 100

New Bicycle, 169

New Coat for Anna, A, 155

Oak Tree, The, 108

Peanut Butter, 44

Song of the Dragon, 143

Spring in China, 157

Two Loaves, 96

Why Coyote Isn't Blue, 118

*boldface indicates how the selections are correlated to activities in the Teacher's Guide.

•INDEX BY CATEGORY•

STORIES

All of Our Noses Are Here, 58
Annie's Pet, 47

Banza, The, 128
Birthday Basket for Tía, A, 140
Bit by Bit, 200

Caps for Sale, 8
Clocks and More Clocks, 167
Couldn't We Have a Turtle Instead?, 26
Crickets, The, 73

Doorbell Rang, The, 193

Enormous Turnip, The, 64

Hattie and the Fox, 21
Hot Thirsty Day, A, 162
How Big Is a Foot?, 152
How Many Ways Can You Cut a Pie?, 189

Jesse Bear, What Will You Wear?, 40

Knee-High Man, The, 98

Leopard Finds Gold, 123
List, A, 105

Maxie, 170
Mexicali Soup, 80
Mitten, The, 4
Moira's Birthday, 50
Morris Goes to School, 100
Most Wonderful Egg in the World, The, 113
Mud for Sale, 91

New Coat for Anna, A, 154
Ninety-Nine Pockets, 158

Oak Tree, The, 108

Penelope Gets Wheels, 149

Snow Parade, The, 179
Story Snail, The, 135

Tatum's Favorite Shape, 33
Thousand Pails of Water, A, 145
Too Many Books!, 198
Too Many Hopkins, 116
Too Much Noise, 14
Two Greedy Bears, 37
Two Hundred Rabbits, 174
Two Loaves, 96

Village of Round and Square Houses, The, 183

Who Wants One?, 61
Why Coyote Isn't Blue, 118

POEMS

Animals' Houses, 115
Ants at the Olympics, The, 89

Band-Aids, 120
Bleezer's Ice Cream, 86

Cats, 3
Cats of Kilkenny, The, 71
Chook, Chook, Chook, 76
Cottage, 104
Counting Rhyme, A, 31
Creature in the Classroom, The, 75

Don't Ask Me, 148

Face of the Clock, The, 110
Fifteen Cents, 94
Five Brown Teddies, 70

Graceful Elephant, The, 66

Homework Machine, 144
Hugs and Kisses, 88

Little Fish, 19

Marrog, The, 121
Money's Funny, 43

New Bicycle, 169

Okay Everybody, 28
One, Two, Buckle My Shoe, 54

Poem for a Pickle, A, 93

Square as a House, 36
Sum, A, 192
Surprises, 182

Ten Little Squirrels, 195
There are Big Waves, 11
There Was an Old Man Who Said, 133
There Was an Old Man with a Beard, 132
There Were Two Wrens, 72
Three Little Monkeys, 49
Too Many Daves, 53

Using Subtraction, 166

What Is Pink?, 12

SONGS

Ai Hai Yo, 112
All Who Born in January, 173

Counting Song, 60

Draw a Bucket of Water, 24

Five Fat Turkeys, 134
Five Little Ducks, 68

Going over the Sea, 55

Harvest, 2
Hello Song, 13
Hokey Pokey, 7
Hop Up, My Ladies, 196
Hot Cross Buns, 151
Hurry, Little Pony, 32

If You're Happy, 20

Johnny Works with One Hammer, 67

Over in the Meadow, 29

Peanut Butter, 44
Pop Goes the Weasel, 95

Song of the Dragon, 143
Spring in China, 157
Spring Is Coming, 97

Ten in a Bed, 78
Ten Little Fingers, 77
Ten Puppies (*Diez Perritos*), 85
This Old Man, 63

Who Has the Penny?, 46

•INDEX BY AUTHOR•

Anderson, Lonzo and Adams, Adrienne, 174

Bauer, Caroline Feller, 198
Baylor, Byrd, 118
Blair, Lee, 166
Brenner, Barbara, 47, 179

Carlstrom, Nancy White, 40
Carroll, Lewis, 192
Champeau, Mary Pat, 123
Coats, Laura Jane, 108

Delacre, Lulu, 66
dePaola, Tomie, 116
Digance, Richard, 89

Farjeon, Eleanor, 3, 11, 104
Fox, Mem, 21

Ginsburg, Mirra, 37
Griego, Margot C., Bucks, Betsy L., Gilbert,
  Sharon S., and Kimball, Laurel H., 19
Grifalconi, Ann, 183

Heine, Helme, 113
Hitte, Kathyrn and Hayes, William D., 80
Hoberman, Mary Ann, 43
Hutchins, Pat, 167, 193

Kantrowitz, Mildred, 170
Kaye, Milton, 97
Kuskin, Karla, 28, 36

Lear, Edward, 132
Lester, Julius, 98
Lobel, Arnold, 73, 105

McGinley, Phyllis, 110
McGovern, Ann, 14
Merriam, Eve, 93
Moncure, Jane Belk, 189
Mora, Pat, 140
Munsch, Robert, 50

Myller, Rolf, 152
Myrick, Jean, 158

Nave, Yolanda, 148, 169
Nelson, Brenda, 91

Parkinson, Kathy, 64
Peterson, Esther Allen, 149
Pomerantz, Charlotte, 88
Prelutsky, Jack, 75, 86

Raffi, 68
Rees, Mary, 78
Reeves, James, 115
Roubidoux, Noel, 118
Rockwell, Anne, 135
Rockwell, Harlow, 96
Rossetti, Christina, 12
Roy, Ronald, 145

Schwartz, Alvin, 58
Scriven, R. C., 121
Serfozo, Mary, 61
Seuss, Dr., 53
Sharmat, Marjorie Weinman, 162
Silverstein, Shel, 120, 144
Slobodkina, Esphyr, 8
Soule, Jean Conder, 182
Stephenson, M. M., 31

Thole, Dorothy, 33
Tresselt, Alvin, 4

Vigna, Judith, 26

Wiseman, B., 100
Wolkstein, Diane, 128

Yount, Lisa, 200

Ziefert, Harriet, 154

•INDEX OF SELECTIONS BY CONTINENT•

AFRICA

The Cameroons

Village of Round and Square Houses, The, 183
By Ann Grifalconi

Niger

Leopard Finds Gold, 123
Retold by Mary Pat Champeau

ASIA

China

Ai Hai Yo, 112

Song of the Dragon, 143

Spring in China, 157

Japan

Thousand Pails of Water, A, 145
By Ronald Roy

AUSTRALIA

Hattie and the Fox, 21
By Mem Fox

EUROPE

Denmark

Harvest, 2

England

Animals' Houses, 115
By James Reeves

Ants at the Olympics, The, 89
By Richard Digance

Cats, 3
By Eleanor Farjeon

Cats of Kilkenny, The, 71

Chook, Chook, Chook, 76

Clocks and More Clocks, 167
By Pat Hutchins

Cottage, 104
By Eleanor Farjeon

Counting Rhyme, A, 31
By M. M. Stephenson

Doorbell Rang, The, 193
By Pat Hutchins

Five Brown Teddies, 70

Hot Cross Buns, 151

One, Two, Buckle My Shoe, 54

Sum, A, 192
By Lewis Carroll

Ten in a Bed, 78
Adapted by Mary Rees

Ten Little Squirrels, 195

There are Big Waves, 11
By Eleanor Farjeon

There Was an Old Man Who Said, 133

There Was an Old Man with a Beard, 132
By Edward Lear

There Were Two Wrens, 72

This Old Man, 63

Three Little Monkeys, 49

What Is Pink?, 12
By Christina Rossetti

Germany

Most Wonderful Egg in the World, The, 113
By Helme Heine

Hungary

Two Greedy Bears, 37
By Mirra Ginsburg

Russia

Enormous Turnip, The, 64
Retold by Kathy Parkinson

Spain

Hurry, Little Pony, 32

Ukraine

Mitten, The, 4
Retold by Alvin Tresselt

NORTH AMERICA

African American

Draw a Bucket of Water, 24

Knee-High Man, The, 98
Retold by Julius Lester

Canada

Going over the Sea, 55

Moira's Birthday, 50
By Robert Munsch

Haiti

Banza, The, 128
By Diane Wolkstein

Mexico

Birthday Basket for Tía, A, 140
By Pat Mora

Counting Song, 60

Graceful Elephant, The, 66
Retold by Lulu Delacre

Little Fish, 19
Translated by Margot C. Griego, Betsy L. Bucks,
    Sharon S. Gilbert, and Laurel H. Kimball

Native American

Why Coyote Isn't Blue, 118
Retold by Noel Roubidoux, collected by Byrd Baylor

Puerto Rico

Ten Puppies (*Diez Perritos*), 85

Trinidad

All Who Born in January, 173

North American Contemporary

All of Our Noses Are Here, 58
Retold by Alvin Schwartz

Annie's Pet, 47
By Barbara Brenner

Band-Aids, 120
By Shel Silverstein

Banza, The, 128
By Diane Wolkstein

Birthday Basket for Tía, A, 140
By Pat Mora

Bit by Bit, 200
By Lisa Yount

Bleezer's Ice Cream, 86
By Jack Prelutsky

Caps for Sale, 8
By Esphyr Slobodkina

Couldn't We Have a Turtle Instead?, 26
By Judith Vigna

Creature in the Classroom, The, 75
By Jack Prelutsky

Crickets, The, 73
By Arnold Lobel

Don't Ask Me, 148
By Yolanda Nave

Enormous Turnip, The, 64
Retold by Kathy Parkinson

Face of the Clock, The, 110
By Phyllis McGinley

Five Little Ducks, 68
By Raffi

Hot Thirsty Day, A, 162
By Marjorie Weinman Sharmat

Homework Machine, 144
By Shel Silverstein

How Big Is a Foot?, 152
By Rolf Myller

How Many Ways Can You Cut a Pie?, 189
By Jane Belk Moncure

Hugs and Kisses, 88
By Charlotte Pomerantz

Jesse Bear, What Will You Wear?, 40
By Nancy White Carlstrom

Knee-High Man, The, 98
Retold by Julius Lester

Leopard Finds Gold, 123
Retold by Mary Pat Champeau

List, A, 105
By Arnold Lobel

Little Fish, 19
Translated by Margot C. Griego, Betsy L. Bucks
    Sharon S. Gilbert, and Laurel H. Kimball

Marrog, The, 121
By R. C. Scriven

Mitten, The, 4
Retold by Alvin Tresselt

Maxie, 170
By Mildred Kantrowitz

Mexicali Soup, 80
By Kathryn Hitte and William D. Hayes

Moira's Birthday, 50
By Robert Munsch

Money's Funny, 43
By Mary Ann Hoberman

Morris Goes to School, 100
By B. Wiseman

Mud for Sale, 91
By Brenda Nelson

New Bicycle, 169
By Yolanda Nave

New Coat for Anna, A, 154
By Harriet Ziefert

Ninety-Nine Pockets, 158
By Jean Myrick

Oak Tree, The, 108
By Laura Jane Coats

Okay Everybody, 28
By Karla Kuskin

Peanut Butter, 44

Penelope Gets Wheels, 149
By Esther Allen Peterson

Poem for a Pickle, A, 93
By Eve Merriam

Snow Parade, The, 179
By Barbara Brenner

Spring Is Coming, 97
By Milton Kaye

Square as a House, 36
By Karla Kuskin

Story Snail, The, 135
By Anne Rockwell

Surprises, 182
By Jean Conder Soule

Tatum's Favorite Shape, 33
By Dorothy Thole

Too Many Books!, 198
By Caroline Feller Bauer

Too Many Daves, 53
By Dr. Seuss

Too Many Hopkins, 116
By Tomie dePaola

Too Much Noise, 14
By Ann McGovern

Two Greedy Bears, 37
Retold by Mirra Ginsburg

Two Hundred Rabbits, 174
By Lonzo Anderson and Adrienne Adams

Two Loaves, 96
By Harlow Rockwell

Using Subtraction, 166
By Lee Blair

Village of Round and Square Houses, The, 183
By Ann Grifalconi

Who Wants One?, 61
By Mary Serfozo

North American Traditional

Fifteen Cents, 94

Five Fat Turkeys, 134

Hello Song, 13

Hokey Pokey, 7

Hop Up, My Ladies, 196

If You're Happy, 20

Johnny Works with One Hammer, 67

Over in the Meadow, 29

Pop Goes the Weasel, 95

Ten Little Fingers, 77

Who Has the Penny?, 46

SOUTH AMERICA

Mexicali Soup, 80
By Kathryn Hitte and William D. Hayes

ACKNOWLEDGMENTS *(continued)*

KATHRYN HITTE HAYES
MEXICALI SOUP by Kathryn Hitte and William D. Hayes. Copyright © 1970 by Kathryn Hitte and William D. Hayes. Reprinted by permission of Kathryn Hitte Hayes.

HENRY HOLT AND COMPANY, INC.
"Little Fish" from TORTILLITAS PARA MAMA AND OTHER NURSERY RHYMES selected and translated by Margot C. Griego, Betsy L. Bucks, Sharon S. Gilbert and Laurel H. Kimball. Copyright © 1981 by Margot Griego, Betsy Bucks, Sharon Gilbert and Laurel Kimball. Reprinted by arrangement with Henry Holt and Company, Inc.

HOUGHTON MIFFLIN CO.
TOO MUCH NOISE by Ann McGovern. Text copyright © 1967 by Ann McGovern.

MUD FOR SALE by Brenda Nelson. Text copyright © 1984 by Brenda Nelson.

Both are reprinted by permission of Houghton Mifflin Company.

LELAND B. JACOBS
"Using Subtraction" by Lee Blair from ARITHMETIC IN VERSE AND RHYME selected by Allan D. Jacobs and Leland B. Jacobs. Reprinted by permission of Leland B. Jacobs.

MICHAEL JOSEPH LTD.
"The Ants at the Olympics" from ANIMAL ALPHABET by Richard Digance. © Richard Dignance 1980. Published by Michael Joseph Ltd. and used with their permission.

MILTON KAYE
"Spring is Coming" by Milton Kaye. Used by permission of the composer.

LANTERN PRESS, INC.
NINETY-NINE POCKETS by Jean Myrick. Copyright © 1966 by Jean Myrick. Reprinted by permission of Lantern Press, Inc.

LITTLE, BROWN AND COMPANY
THE VILLAGE OF ROUND AND SQUARE HOUSES by Ann Grifalconi. Copyright © 1986 by Ann Grifalconi.

TEN IN A BED by Mary Rees. Copyright © 1988 by Mary Rees.

Both are by permission of Little, Brown and Company.

GINA MACCOBY LITERARY AGENCY
"Money's Funny" from NUTS TO YOU AND NUTS TO ME by Mary Ann Hoberman. Copyright © 1974 by Mary Ann Hoberman. Reprinted by permission of Gina Maccoby Literary Agency.

MACMILLAN PUBLISHING COMPANY
"Jesse Bear, What Will You Wear?" from JESSE BEAR, WHAT WILL YOU WEAR? by Nancy White Carlstrom. Copyright © 1986 by Nancy White Carlstrom.

"Leopard Finds Gold" by Mary Pat Champeau.

"The Oak Tree" from THE OAK TREE by Laura Jane Coats. Copyright © 1987 by Laura Jane Coats and Macmillan Publishing Co.

"Hattie and the Fox" from HATTIE AND THE FOX by Mem Fox. Copyright © 1986 by Mem Fox. By permission of Bradbury Press, an affiliate of Macmillan, Inc.

"Two Greedy Bears" from TWO GREEDY BEARS by Mirra Ginsburg. Copyright © 1976 by Mirra Ginsburg.